WILLIAM McKINLEY

AN INSPIRING BIOGRAPHY

by

EVA HIGGINS

DARING PUBLISHING GROUP, INC.
DARING BOOKS • LIFE ENRICHMENT PUBLISHERS
CANTON • OHIO

Published by Daring Books
P.O. Box 20050, Canton, Ohio 44701

Library of Congress Cataloging-in-Publication Data

Higgins, Eva, 1928-
William McKinley : an inspiring biography / by Eva Higgins
p. cm.
Includes bibliographical references.
Summary: A biography of the twenty-fifth president, reflecting his politics, his philosophy, and events of his term.
ISBN 0-938936-89-1
1. McKinley, William, 1843-1901--Juvenile literature.
2. Presidents--United States--Biography--Juvenile literature.
[1. McKinley, William, 1843-1901. 2. Presidents.] I. Title.
E711.6.H54 1989
973.8'8'092--dc20
[B]
[92] 89-27581
CIP
AC

10 9 8 7 6 5 4 3 2 1

Printed in the United States of America.

Dedication

This book is dedicated to

my grandmother,

Kitty Young Sheely Schaedler

and

my mother,

Leota Richards

Table of Contents

Foreword

Eva Higgins' book, William McKinley, is an intriguing profile unshrouding the essence of the 25th President of the United States. It is a story of pioneer hardship, love, humility, diplomacy, compassion, diligence, faith, tolerance, and respect for others. This book is intended for young readers (10 years old and up) and for any person who wants a succinct overview of McKinley's life, politics, philosophy, and some of the world problems during his time.

McKinley's early life was frugal, but filled with family love and support. This gave him a positive outlook and an ability to care for others. He learned to take pride in fulfilling his responsibilities, in his appearance and morals. These attributes gave him the impetus to succeed. His personal pride was contrasted by a humility too great to permit the development of vanity.

The years he spent in politics show him to have been an outstanding diplomat whose primary interest was for the welfare of others. His concern for the South, Southerners, Filipinos, Cubans, Puerto Ricans and American Indians attest to his respect for the rights of others.

The twenty-eight years he spent caring for an invalid wife, the feats he performed in the Shenandoah Valley, the nurturing he provided for an orphaned niece and nephew, the worry that plagued him over the fate of Americans during the Spanish-American War: all demonstrated his deep compassion for and loyalty to his fellow man.

His tolerance toward religions other than his own, towards schoolmates who called him, "Fatty," toward striking workers, and even toward Spain during the Cuban crisis, were the hallmarks of a temperate and tolerant man.

However, because he could never hurt anyone else, it never occurred to him that others would intentionally hurt him. He paid for this innocent trust—once financially, and eventually with his life.

The real McKinley is revealed in this unique and enlightening biography.

Dennis Bartow, Publisher

1

Humble Beginnings

William McKinley Jr., the twenty-fifth President of the United States, was never as wealthy as George Washington and not nearly as tall as Abraham Lincoln, but many believe that he ranks with these two men in his contributions to the United States.

George Washington organized the plans for freedom of self-government for the American people.

Abraham Lincoln preserved this freedom when it was seriously threatened during the Civil War.

William McKinley, patiently and wisely, guided the United States from the status of an immature, isolated country to that of a powerful one with responsibilities among all the nations of the world.

McKinley's ancestors were hard-working Scotch-Irish people who embraced the self-discipline of both Quaker and Methodist churches. Two of his great-grandfathers defended America in the Revolutionary War and in the War of 1812, just as their Scotch ancestors had fought

Illustration by Mary Miller

President William McKinley Jr., twenty-fifth president of the United States.

to save their homes in the Caledonian Mountain Highlands from greedy Lowland barons.

These highlanders passed on to their descendants a fierce loyalty to home, family, and country, tempered by love and respect for their fellow men and God.

William McKinley Jr. inherited these qualities when he was born in Niles, Ohio, January 29, 1843, to William McKinley Sr. and Nancy Campbell Allison.

* * * * *

William McKinley Sr. began to work with his father when he was sixteen years old. They managed blast furnaces to produce pig iron from raw iron ore. The men had to chop wood for the furnace fires, dig the iron ore out of mines with a pick, load it on a wagon and unload it into the furnace. The work demanded a great deal of knowledge about horses, their care and their harnesses. Wagons had to be kept in good repair in order to transport the pig iron to market.

Despite long hours of hard work, William McKinley Sr. found time to study. His only education had come from the small country school he attended as a child and he was eager to learn more. He kept three books with him to study when he found a spare moment: the Bible, Shakespeare, and Dante.

In 1829 he married Nancy Campbell Allison, a childhood schoolmate. Nancy was one of nine children that Abner and Ann (Campbell) Allison reared in New Lisbon (now Lisbon), Ohio.

The Allisons' ancestors had come to America from

Scotland and Nancy lived and taught her children the values of her Scotch family. Her close attention to the details of healthy, common-sense living allowed her to rear eight of her nine children without the benefit of water piped into her home, a washing machine or a furnace. Only one baby, Abigail Celia, died as an infant in these nearly primitive conditions.

Nancy was a pious woman who worshipped and reared her children according to the strict religious principles of the Methodist church. She and her sister, Mrs. Jacob Reep, took care of the Methodist church in Niles. They swept the floors, dusted the pews, supplied fuel, and found food and lodging for the itinerant preachers who came to spread the Word of God.

In this church, taboos existed for almost every worldly pleasure. Dancing, playing cards and attending theater plays were all considered evils which caused shiftlessness. One minister shouted at his blushing congregation that dancing was nothing but "huggin' up . . . two strangers huggin' up."

To Nancy, 'shiftlessness' was "cousin to drink," and drink was evil and destructive. She believed everyone should work their land "smartly," take care of their barns and equipment, and keep a properly stocked food pantry. She made sure everybody worked, "with a sense of unity," and family pride.

Despite her strict insistence on living such a clean life, this strong-willed, thrifty woman nurtured love and devotion in all of her children. She seemed especially close to her next youngest child, William Jr., and fostered the hope that he would one day be a minister.

Though young William didn't fulfill her wish, he was a devout church member from the time he humbly marched to the "mourner's bench" where he promised to follow the teachings of Christ. He was ten years old when he made this commitment and for the remainder of his life, he worked to fulfill it.

William Sr. and Nancy McKinley had nine children.

David - born 1830, died 1892. He was Consul to Honolulu for a time, and later, Minister to Hawaii.

Anna - born 1832, died July 29, 1890. She was a schoolteacher and principal of a school in Canton, Ohio for more than thirty years. Buried in Westlawn Cemetery, Canton, Ohio. See Memorials, Chapter 12.

James - born 1834, died 1889. Lived and worked in California and New Castle, Pennsylvania. Buried in Westlawn Cemetery, Canton, Ohio.

Mary - born 1836, died 1869. Married Daniel May and lived in Poland, Ohio.

Helen - born 1838, died June 9, 1924. Schoolteacher. Moved to Cleveland after her mother died in 1897.

Sarah Elizabeth - born 1840, died November 22, 1931. Married Andrew J. Duncan and lived in Cleveland, Ohio. Buried in Poland, Ohio near sister, Mary McKinley May.

William Jr. - born January 29, 1843, died September 14, 1901. Attorney and twenty-fifth President of the United States.

Abigail ‘‘Abbie’’ Celia - born 1845, died January 6, 1846.

Abner - born 1847, died 1904. Lawyer and partner of William. Lived in Canton, Ohio, New York and Pennsylvania.

Illustration by Mary Miller

Birthplace of William McKinley, Jr., Niles, Ohio.

2

Bare Feet and Old Sow

Niles, Ohio was very small when the McKinleys lived there. It was an isolated frontier town with three hundred people when William McKinley Jr. was four years old in 1847.

Split-rail fences, covered with climbing wild roses, separated most fields and farms. The thorny roses usually kept the pigs, cows, and sheep inside their own pasture fields except when an itching or inquisitive animal knocked the gate rails down. Then the critters escaped to create a thundering, bleating, oinking havoc until they were herded back home.

There was a canal, no railroad, and one wagon trail to Pittsburgh, Pennsylvania. There were three stores, one of them in the McKinleys' frame home on the main street of town. The McKinley family helped tend the store which occupied a room at the left front corner of their long, narrow house. In addition to the stores, there were three churches and five businesses, including

Mr. McKinley's blast furnace.

William Jr. was a serious, stocky boy who always wanted to do his homework before he played games with his friends. Young McKinley said he enjoyed playing only when he knew his work was finished. One of his favorite games was "Old Sow," a game like golf where a stick was used to hit a block of wood into a hole.

Following the Mexican War, the young boys often played soldier. With paper hats and stick swords, they marched around the banks of Mosquito Creek and charged from behind rocks and bushes to make their pretend attacks.

One summer when William was quite young and didn't know know to swim, he was tempted by the cool sparkling water in Mosquito Creek and went "swimming" with a friend, Joseph G. Butler Jr. William began to sink and Butler tried to save him—but he couldn't swim either. Both boys were going down for the third time when a young man named Jacob Shealer, jumped in and dragged them to safety.

When William Jr. was an adult, he recalled that the most luxurious feeling he'd ever known had occurred in a barren meadow in Niles, Ohio. He often went barefoot to bring the cows from the pasture field to the barn. In winter, when his feet were cold, he snuggled them into the warm earth where one of the cows had been lying.

William Sr. and Nancy McKinley were far from

wealthy. He worked long hard hours at his foundry and Nancy made sure his meager income was used wisely to fill the needs of their large family. Providing food, warmth, and education, along with the disciplines of cleanliness for body and soul, were the goals of these parents.

William Jr. knew at an early age that his parents wanted more education for their children than the school in Niles offered, thus it came as no surprise when he learned the family would move closer to Youngstown so the children could attend high school.

He was nine years old in 1852 when they packed their clothes and household goods into wagons and moved ten miles south of Niles to Poland, Ohio. Here the Methodist high school, Poland Union Seminary, was located. William Sr. remained in Niles to manage his foundry and visited his family on weekends. Nancy solved the daily problems of rearing a family alone.

The town of Poland wasn't much larger than Niles, but was described as one of the neatest villages in Ohio. Its one hundred homes were nearly all painted white. William liked to poke around at nearby Beaver Creek, his favorite spot for fishing and camping in the summer, and ice skating in the winter.

Young William liked the school where he soon learned he had special talents for both public speaking and debate. He was so popular with his classmates that they elected him to be the first president of Poland Seminary's Everett Literary and Debating Society.

One of his fellow students said, "Will is good at everything he goes at," but respect did not keep them from making fun of him. In grade school, they called him "Fatty," and at Poland Seminary, the "barefooted orator," because he insisted that nobody could wear their "dirty" shoes on the carpet in the debate room. He ignored the teasing—he loved his childhood playmates, and every debate at Poland Seminary was conducted by high school students in their stocking feet while young McKinley attended the school.

When William Jr. was seventeen years old, he graduated from Poland Seminary, then enrolled in Allegheny College in Meadville, Pennsylvania. Before the first school term ended, however, illness forced him to return home. His friends at school said he was sick because he studied too much and didn't get enough rest.

By the time he was well enough to return to school several months later, money was more scarce than it had been earlier. The family business was on a decline because the Panic of 1857 had left the nation in a depression. William decided to get a job to pay for his own tuition.

He was hired to teach one term in the Kerr District School in Poland and when school was out, he clerked at the Poland Post Office.

During this time the slavery argument between newly elected President Abraham Lincoln and the southern slave states worsened. Seven states withdrew from the Union and formed the Confederate States of America to preserve slavery in their "independent" nation.

President Lincoln announced that this Confederacy of southern states was not legal. He sent supplies to Fort Sumter at Charleston, South Carolina in an effort to keep possession of this federal garrison. But the Confederates dug in, fought and forced the Union garrison to surrender on April 14, 1861, after a battle which lasted just thirty-six hours.

President Lincoln responded to this insult to the Union by calling for troops to enforce the laws of the United States. Mass public meetings were quickly called together to enlist volunteers for three months of service.

William McKinley Jr. and his cousin and friend, William McKinley Osborne, attended one of those patriotic meetings in Poland in early May. The meeting aroused the boys' patriotism, but they did not enlist in a state of wild emotion. They calmly travelled to Youngstown to see the first enlistees off, talked the situation over during their drive, and decided they would join the Union Army. Neither of them knew what lay ahead.

Illustration by Mary Miller

William McKinley, Jr., a soldier in the Civil War, age 22.

3

Private to Brevet Major

The feelings these teenagers shared can be understood from parts of a speech William Jr. made twenty-eight years later on May 30, 1889 to the Grand Army of the Republic in the Metropolitan Opera House in New York. The speech was titled: *The American Volunteer Soldier*, and McKinley said:

"They enlisted in the Army with no expectation of promotion; not for the paltry pittance of pay; not for fame of popular applause, for their services, however efficient, were not to be heralded abroad. They entered the Army moved by the highest and purest motives of patriotism, that no harm might befall the Republic. . . .

"We counted no cost when the war commenced. We knew little of the great sacrifices which were to come or the scope and extent of that great war—we only knew that the nation of our fathers was in danger by the hand of treason . . . It was then that the genius of self-government asserted itself and the whole nation was turned into a camp for muster and military instruction. The citizens voluntarily came together to join an army bound together in a common cause for common purpose—the preservation of the Union. It was an awful experience for the American boy, who knew nothing of war, in many instances, save as he read of it in the glamour of history . . . unused to hardships, unaccustomed to toil, undrilled in the tactics of war.

With a mother's blessing and a father's affectionate farewell, he went forth with firm resolve to give up all, even the last drop of life's blood, that this nation should be saved."

In June, 1861, William McKinley Jr. said good-bye to his bravely tearful mother and loving father, with the confident promise that he would return home alive and well. A few days later he and his cousin arrived at Fort Chase near Columbus, Ohio, where they learned that the three-month-service quota was filled. They promptly enlisted in Company E of the 23rd Ohio Volunteer Infantry for three years or the duration, whichever would be needed.

Sanitary conditions of the camps were very poor and young Osborne was one of many soldiers who soon became ill. He was discharged November 4, 1861, but William McKinley Jr. remained to serve four years in the Union Army. His submission to discipline and hardship, along with his calm self-assurance and dependability, made him a respected soldier.

William was a private when the blue-uniformed men of the 23rd left Ohio on July 25, 1861, to zig-zag their way on primitive roads through swamps, farms and forests to Clarksburg, Virginia (now West Virginia). For the next two months these men dragged heavy guns and prodded horses and wagons over rugged mountain terrain day and night. They were often soaked by rains while they fought itchy and painful battles with mosquitoes, deerflies, chiggers, and ticks, and engaged in small skirmishes with scattered bands of Confederate soldiers.

McKinley's cheerful outlook was recorded in a letter he wrote to his cousin, W. K. Miller, that summer. He described a "very nice place for encampment on one of Virginia's delightful hills" surrounded by the Western Branch of the Monongahela River, where "we have some fine times. . . ."

His sense of humor was obvious when he gave an amusing description of a night patrol. It seems the men heard rattling pebbles and immediately thought that rebel soldiers were stealing about in the dark. One energetic young lieutenant poked vigorously into some bushes with his "gilded sword" to chase the "sesechers" out but jabbed a skunk instead. A humbled group quickly retreated from a smelly situation.

William stood guard in a corn field for the rest of the night with his old musket primed and ready to shoot any secessionists who might show their faces. He was rewarded only with grunting hogs and frisking young calves.

Young McKinley, with his bushy eyebrows and deeply clefted chin, was well-liked by his fellow soldiers, and in return, he thoroughly enjoyed the gaiety and fellowship they offered.

His home environment had been frugal and humble, but the security and happiness of that childhood gave him both optimism and the ability to feel a warm affection for others.

Miller had offered to send McKinley anything he

needed; however, when William wrote back he asked only for newspapers. He had no money and few postage stamps, but his main interest was in keeping himself informed about current events. Fellow soldiers said he spent most of his leisure time reading papers and always knew the progress of the war.

On September 10, 1861, McKinley saw his first serious military action at Carnifex Ferry, West Virginia, in a tough battle with some rebel irregulars. During the battle he proved to be a good soldier who did not complain about hardship. He was not careless or irresponsible, but seemed calmly certain that nothing would happen to him, and he moved about the battlefield confidently. He said later that this battle "gave us confidence in ourselves and faith in our commander. We learned that we could fight and whip the rebels on their own ground."

The regiment spent the remainder of the winter in the routines of drilling and recruiting. The regiment's Lieutenant Colonel Rutherford B. Hayes, a lawyer from Cincinnati, noticed and liked the way William McKinley handled his duties that winter. In April, 1862, he promoted the young private to commissary sergeant. William quietly went about learning his new duties and keeping records in his neat, precise way for the commanding officers.

Between April 22 and August 15, 1862, the regiment was involved in many skirmishes around East River, then Flat Top Mountain where they nearly starved. On

August 15, they were ordered to Camp Piatt on the Great Kanawha River at the greatest possible speed. They arrived three days later, having marched 104 miles. This was one of the fastest marches on record for such a large body of men.

Transports took them by river to Parkersburg where they boarded a train for Washington D.C., then marched the rest of the way to join the army of General McClellan in Maryland. During this march, young William had his first view of the National Capital, a city threatened by Confederate Grays that waited to be rescued by this marching throng in blue from the North.

When McKinley's regiment reached Frederick, Maryland, they drove the Confederates out, then went to Middletown, reaching it on September 13. The following day the Battle of South Mountain began. This encounter escalated into the Battle of Antietam, Sept. 17, 1862, one of the bloodiest scenes of the entire war.

On this deadly battlefield, McKinley, who was in charge of his brigade's supplies, realized by late afternoon that the men, in battle since dawn, had to be hungry and thirsty. He asked some straggling soldiers to help him load two wagons with hot meat and coffee. They hitched a team of mules to each wagon and set out toward the battlefield. When one team became disabled, McKinley found a stray pair, hooked them to the wagon, and calmly but carefully urged them through the flying missiles to get food and drink to the men of his brigade.

McKinley described what he saw later. "The Colors (Flag) of the regiment were riddled and the blue field almost completely carried away by shells and bullets."

When the battle was over and more than twenty thousand soldiers who had been killed or wounded were cared for, the men began to praise McKinley for his bravery in delivering food to them. The young man was extremely modest, never vain or proud, but he did not underestimate his accomplishments or his ability.

When he found the opportunity, he asked Colonel Hayes' brother-in-law to tell Hayes that he would not refuse a promotion if anyone saw fit to offer it.

So it was, when William went home in the autumn of 1862 on the only leave he received during his four years in service, he wore new second lieutenant bars. Family members later said he "bubbled over with enthusiasm" when he told them about his experiences. This visible excitement was unusual for William who in later years was described as a man who "never gushed with emotion."

Rutherford B. Hayes recalled the performance of McKinley in an address at Lakeside, Ohio, July 30, 1891. He said,

> ". . . From his hands every man in the regiment was served with hot coffee and warm meats, a thing that had never occurred under similar circumstances in any other army in the world. He passed under fire and delivered, with his own hands, these things so essential for the men for whom he was laboring."

When William returned to the regiment after this leave, his officer's duties brought him in closer contact with Colonel Hayes, who was most impressed with the conduct of this young man. Hayes made a note in his diary dated December 13, 1862, that said, "Our new Second Lieutenant McKinley returned today—an exceedingly bright, intelligent and gentlemanly young officer. He promises to be one of the best."

The letters Hayes wrote home also spoke highly of William, whom he described as: "a handsome, bright, gallant boy," and "one of the bravest and finest officers in the army."

William, in turn, found his place as an assistant to the Colonel more suitable to his personality than bloody turf. He was not naturally hostile or quarrelsome, but was cool and courteous, and liked to do things in a systematic way. He became an expert horseman in command of Company D and in February, 1863, was promoted to first lieutenant.

During that winter the regiments remained at the Falls of the Great Kanawha River. They were not called for active duty again until July, 1863.

At that time, a fiesty group of over two thousand volunteers under the leadership of John Morgan, called "Morgan's Raiders," had broken through Union lines in Kentucky and were conducting raids in southern Indiana and Ohio.

They took prisoners, burned bridges, and stole horses and whatever else they wanted, including food.

Housewives had freshly baked bread, drying noodles, and plucked chickens stolen, but the ladies were more worried about their animals. The women and children often hid horses in strange places to keep them from Morgan's Raiders. Sometimes they rode them deep into the woods where undergrowth was thick, in the hope that the soldiers wouldn't bother with a time-consuming ride to look for them. Others hid the horses in their homes or under big piles of hay.

Hayes volunteered to stop these raids. His troops headed the aggressive cavalrymen off at Buffington's Island in the Ohio River where John Morgan was finally captured and imprisoned in Columbus, Ohio.

The 23rd did no more fighting until the spring of 1864, when ordered to join General Crook for a raid on the Virginia and Tennessee Railroad. McKinley was now first lieutenant of Company E—the old Poland Company. His own words best describe this experience:

> "It was a rough and trying march, over mountains and through deep ravines and dense woods, with snows and rains that would have checked the advance of any but the most determined. Daily we were brought in contact with the enemy. We penetrated a country where guerrillas were abundant and where it was not an unusual thing for our own men to be shot from the underbrush—murdered in cold blood."

This long, hard march ended in the Battle of Cloyd Mountain, May 9, 1864, where the 23rd displayed its bravery by advancing steadily on the Confederates until it was so close that the Union men were able to capture two pieces of artillery. The Confederates were beaten after they made three unsuccessful attempts to defend themselves against the men in blue.

More traveling and more fighting followed. They forded swollen streams, struggled through mud and rain and nearly starved before finally reaching Stanton, Virginia, June 8. From there they pushed on past Brownsburg and Lexington to Lynchburg, where another fight took place.

The men had no sleep and little food. Many fell asleep on their feet and their equally exhausted comrades struggled to drag them along. Finally, on June 27, after a nine-day march of 180 miles, they met a supply train on Big Sewall Mountain.

Here the men "stopped and ate, marched and ate, camped about dark and ate all night." They reached Charleston, West Virginia, July 1, 1864, rested for ten days, then were ordered to stop the Confederate raids in Maryland and Pennsylvania. After yet another fierce battle, the regiments marched through Parkersburg to Martinsburg.

On the march to Martinsburg, William, who had turned twenty-one-years-old on January 29, 1864, voted for the first time. The election booth was an ambulance and the ballot box an empty candle can. McKinley cast his vote to elect Abraham Lincoln to his second term as President of the United States.

July 24, 1864, dawned to witness another ferocious battle near Winchester where McKinley completed one more extraordinary task. During the heaviest fighting,

Col. Hayes discovered that an isolated regiment had not been given the order to retreat and was in danger of being annihilated in an orchard.

Hayes pointed toward the orchard and asked McKinley if he would "be willing to carry an order to the colonel to retreat." Without a word, William jumped on his "little bob-tailed horse and spurred him off across the field." Bullets flew, shells exploded, and his course lay across an open field through the thickest of these exploding missiles.

McKinley and his horse were suddenly enveloped in a cloud of dust and smoke when a shell hit directly in front of them. Hayes said later that he thought his brave young comrade was gone and described what happened.

"The little brown horse soon emerged, with its rider as firmly in the saddle as a cowboy, and on they dashed until they reached the shelter of some trees."

The regiment was saved and McKinley went on to encourage and help the exhausted men of Company E to salvage four abandoned guns with caissons. The next day, he was appointed captain of Company G.

More scattered battles kept them busy from July 20 until September 3, when a spectacular engagement took place at Berryville. This was the Battle of Opequan, near Winchester, another important event for the 23rd Ohio. Young McKinley continued to assert his supervisory abilities at Fisher's Hill and Cedar Creek.

On the recommendations of General Crook and

approved by General Sheridan, young McKinley was made a brevet major of volunteers by President Lincoln, March 13, 1865, before he was mustered out of the service. His commission was signed, "A. Lincoln," for "gallant and meritorious service" in the Shenandoah Valley.

For the rest of his life, friends and acquaintances called him, "Major." Only his closest family members ever called him, "Will."

Major McKinley returned home to a joyful reunion with his anxious parents. He came home without a scratch, just as he'd promised, and it should also be noted that he escaped the infections which raged in the unsanitary army camps. It seems his mother's detailed attention to cleanliness was carefully observed and followed by this diligent son.

Illustration by Mary Miller

Ida Saxton McKinley
Age 24

William McKinley, Jr.
Age 28

4

Vocations and Vows

When William returned to Poland, Ohio, in 1865, he was mature. He was twenty-two years old, had worked hard, and possessed greater muscular strength than ever before in his life. His natural tendency to do what needed to be done, despite any obstacle, had firmed his character. His family and millions of others would come to depend on this man, with his strengths and his sound reasoning, during the next thirty-five years.

McKinley's close association with men of all ranks and from all walks of life during the war had developed the skills of working with people that his early schoolteachers had recognized.

The war experiences also strengthened his political beliefs. From childhood he'd read news accounts carefully and at the age of eighteen years, had believed in Abraham Lincoln's anti-slavery position. The young veteran was even more convinced Lincoln was right.

He had no desire to see the defeated southerners punished, but avidly supported civil rights for the negro, as well as Lincoln's program of reconstruction in the south.

As a young boy, William had spent many content hours in the company of his mother and older sisters where he learned the value of peaceful discussions. His dislike for conflict was heightened by his experiences in the war.

One such experience occurred one day when he made hospital rounds with a Union surgeon. The camaraderie between this Northern doctor and some of the wounded Confederate soldiers had surprised the young McKinley. When he asked about it, he was told that the Union doctor and the Confederate soldiers were brother Masons.

Soon after this William joined the Masons where the ties between men rise above the preconceived suspicions and intolerance of conflict. His unbiased attitudes were evident when he chose to be inducted into Masonry by a Confederate judge in Winchester, Virginia.

When Major McKinley put his uniform away for the last time, he left with it the horrors of battle. He never liked to talk about the atrocities of war publicly, even in speeches when it would have been appropriate.

Images of duty and fellowship were the memories he cared about, and those were what he chose to share with others. He liked the disciplines and rewards of military life, but detested the killing and crippling of people and the destruction of property. This young man firmly believed that open discussions between disputing parties was the only civilized way to settle arguments.

Major McKinley had to get on with his life but he had not learned any profession except the Military. He was offered the post of second lieutenant in the Regular army, which his family frowned upon, and which he decided not to accept.

He didn't feel drawn to the ministry as his mother had hoped, but did feel an interest in politics. He recognized his ability to work with others and believed that his talent to make himself easily understood would be useful in working for peace. He had developed an intense patriotism which he described in the address, *The American Volunteer Soldier*, as follows:

> "My friends, we had a million soldiers in the field when the war terminated, and the highest testimony to their character is found in the fact that when the muster-out came, and that vast army, which for years had been accustomed to war and carnage, returned to their homes, they dropped into the quiet walks of citizenship and no trace of them was ever discernable except in their integrity of character, their intense patriotism, and their participation in the growth and development and maintenance of the Government which they had contributed so much to save."

Those few words express what must have been his feeling of responsibility toward the United States after his war experiences. This sense of duty to his homeland came from the same internal source as his sense of duty to the comrades for whom he risked his life to deliver meat and coffee.

McKinley realized politics was the field that would provide him with the greatest prospect for working toward peace. He also knew he needed to study law in order to compete with politicians.

The Major wasted no time. Before the end of 1865, he was reading law in the Youngstown, Ohio office of Attorney Charles E. Glidden, who soon became Judge Glidden. The young veteran read and studied diligently for just over a year until September 1866, when he enrolled at the Albany Law School in New York.

His roommate at 36 Jay Street in Albany, was George F. Arrell, who became an attorney in Youngstown, Ohio. George described William:

> "He never quarrelled, but he had a mind of his own and was very determined. Even at that time he had made up his mind to enter public life and clearly showed an ambition to go to Congress. He worked very hard, often reading until one or two o'clock in the morning. It was his very great industry, rather than genius, that paved the way for his success."

In October, after William was settled in the routine of school once again, he wrote a letter to Rutherford B. Hayes, whose morals and wisdom he admired. McKinley told Hayes about his plans for the future but the letter Hayes wrote back would have discouraged most younger men:

> "With your business capacity and experience," it said, "I would have preferred Rail Roading or some commercial business. A man in any of our Western towns with half your wit ought to be independent at forty in business. As a lawyer a man sacrifices independence to ambition which is a bad bargain at best."

This advice from Hayes, who was campaigning for a second term in Congress, was wrong, because though McKinley had always prepared neat paperwork for Hayes and was very conscientious in performing his duties, he was too trusting of others to be a successful businessman.

This was proved later when he loaned his early savings to a friend to rescue a failing tin plate business. As the business continued to falter, the man made several return trips for McKinley's signature, which he said were to extend the terms of the original loan. In reality, he was giving McKinley new notes for additional loans.

McKinley was so trusting he never read the secondary notes, and when the business finally did fail, his friend's creditors came to McKinley for one hundred thirty thousand dollars instead of the fifteen thousand McKinley thought he'd loaned.

William was devastated by this treachery of a friend, and the fact that he did not have that kind of money. When the public learned of his problem they sent contributions, which further embarrassed McKinley. A businessman named Marcus Hanna, politician Asa Bushnell, and others paid the bad debts to save McKinley's reputation and his wife's inheritance.

This incident clearly showed McKinley was a generous and trusting person, but was not shrewd enough to be a successful businessman.

The young law student read Hayes's letter carefully.

He knew he could inspire confidence and affection in others and he liked public speaking. With these gifts so much a part of him, William decided to follow Hayes' example instead of his advice. He folded the letter from his mentor and put it in a small tin box with a few other important papers.

Just one year later he was stumping in Ohio, making political speeches to help in Hayes' campaign for governorship of Ohio.

Early in 1867, young McKinley passed the Ohio Bar examination and began his search for a growing town in which to build his law practice. His sister Anna, who was twelve years older than he, was principal of a grammar school in Canton, Ohio, and wanted him to settle there.

In the spring of 1867, he visited her and found friendly people who loved and respected his sister. The town was growing, it was the seat of Stark County and the men who made up the law profession had built a legal bar with a good reputation. William immediately chose Canton as the place to make his home and build his practice.

Anna had helped William attend Albany Law School by adding enough money to his savings to pay his tuition. In Canton, her social contacts proved helpful but William's good looks, quick step, slim, muscled body, and warm smile, quickly made him popular with the residents.

He carried his body erect and people liked the

strength and quality of his low tenor voice. His morals were flawless. He didn't smoke, drink or swear, and treated women with deep respect.

McKinley often laughed at his own inexperience and simplicity and liked to tell about the first time he tasted ice cream. It was during a reception for law students at Albany. He thought the hostess had accidentally frozen the custard, and in later years when he laughed about the incident, he finished by saying, "You know, I was a simple country boy."

This simplicity, or lack of sophistication was an advantage to William in Canton, Ohio in 1867. Canton was a simple, country town and young McKinley was respected as a fine Christian gentleman. He understood perfectly well how useful this image would be in achieving his goals, and felt good about the cleanliness of his body and his life.

The value he placed on these high morals is clearly seen in a letter he wrote to his nephew, James, many years later:

". . . look after your diet and living, take no intoxicants, indulge in no immoral practices. Keep your life and your speech both clean, and be brave."

Major William McKinley Jr. had a natural love for fun but his strict Methodist upbringing left him unable to enjoy idle fun. He once told a friend that he felt self-conscious and simply could not be comfortable dancing or playing cards. He liked children and often chuckled heartily as he watched them at play. He indulged in horseback riding and walking since all other sports were beyond his ability to enjoy.

In later years, he learned to appreciate stage plays, became especially fond of Shakespeare, and played cribbage with his wife.

McKinley was never a loner. He joined many groups, including veteran organizations, the YMCA, Masonic Lodge, the County Republican Committee and the First Methodist Church.

He taught in and became superintendent of the Sunday School in the Canton Methodist church where he was active. This devotion as a Methodist never interfered with his tolerance of other religions. His personal faith was based on a loving and kind God and he had many friends among Canton's numerous Roman Catholic families.

He was concerned about the dangers of alcohol abuse and became active in temperance activities where he often spoke for total abstinence from alcohol.

McKinley first went into politics for himself in 1869 when he ran on the Republican ticket for prosecuting attorney of Stark County. Though the county residents voted Democrat, he won as a Republican, which showed both his popularity and his ability to get votes. This term as prosecutor also revealed his attitude about the illegal sales of liquor.

Alliance, a town about fifteen miles east of Canton, was one of his targets because some saloons sold bootleg liquor, which posed a threat to students of Mt.

Union College. The Major was able to convict these saloon keepers by testimony from some of the students. At this same time, a temperance movement was swiftly growing in the entire nation, and McKinley's local success gave this movement support in Stark County.

From the time William first came to Canton, he and Anna tried to persuade their parents to move from Poland to this thriving town. Their brothers, David and James, had followed an uncle to California while Sarah Elizabeth had married Andrew Duncan and moved to Cleveland. Their sister Helen never married and retired from teaching school to stay with her mother. Abner maintained his home with his parents while he studied law and Mary was married to Daniel May of Poland. When Mary died in 1869, her parents seemed to lose interest in Poland and agreed to move to Canton.

Young William bought a small house near the square at 131 West Tuscarawas Street. His father sold the foundry in Poland, then invested in a furnace in Michigan which he managed for another seven years.

The people of Canton liked the sprightly Nancy Allison McKinley, and were soon calling her, "Mother McKinley." William Junior's devotion to her was well known as he escorted her to church each Sunday and treated her with a deep respect. But Mother McKinley wore a slight frown.

She wasn't happy about her son's political plans, he was smoking cigars on occasion, and a frivolous "city" girl, named, Ida Saxton, was beginning to attract his attention.

The Saxton family was wealthy. James A. Saxton was a Canton banker and businessman, whose father had founded the first newspaper in Canton. James' wife, Katherine DeWalt, also came from an early, well-known Canton family. This couple had the means, and some Cantonians felt they over-indulged their three children, Ida, Mary and George.

Ida and Pina (Mary's nickname was pronounced, Piney) attended Canton Public Schools, a private school in New York and a school in Cleveland, Ohio. In 1867, the Saxtons decided to send their daughters to a finishing school at Brooke Hall Seminary in Media, Pennsylvania—a popular girls' boarding school. Although Ida was past the age when most girls went to this school, she loved it and developed some lifelong friendships while there.

Ida and Pina were "finished" in one year and came back to Canton just as Miss Jeanette Alexander, a Canton schoolteacher, was making arrangements to take some of Canton's young women on a tour of Europe. The Saxton girls joined this tour. Miss Alexander wanted her brother to go along as the group's business manager, but the idea mysteriously failed and the spinster teacher had a miserable eight months in Europe alone with the girls.

According to Miss Alexander, Ida Saxton created most of her misery by going places and doing things "nice" girls didn't do. Once, she and several other girls went to a theater in Paris with some young men they'd barely met, which sent their chaperone into a tizzy.

Jeanette Alexander wrote a letter home blamed Ida for the fact that her brother had not been permitted to go along. She said she knew it was because her brother was not one of Ida's admirers. In her letter, Miss Alexander said, "She set her head he should not come and that earned the day for there is no let up when she does set her head." She noted in her diary that Ida was "headstrong and spoiled."

When the girls returned to Canton, Major McKinley met Ida at a picnic. This first meeting of the lovely, delicate, auburn-haired, blue-eyed Canton maiden and the handsome, popular young attorney apparently didn't stir either of them. There is no record of any dating between them at that time.

Mr. Saxton became concerned about Ida after the girls returned from their European tour. She seemed restless and uneasy, not her usual happy-go-lucky self at all. He decided she needed something to occupy her mind and suggested she come to the bank to learn banking.

Ida agreed, and despite the fact that her education had been geared more toward social graces than mathematical skills, she was keen enough to learn the duties of a bank cashier. It was here that Major McKinley met her the second time.

The lovely young woman who grew up in luxury, learning how always to get her own way, began to tug at the heartstrings of the gentle man whose greatest childhood luxury had been finding a warm spot for his cold bare feet in a winter pasture field.

Ida must have known he was of solid convictions, not capable of fickleness. She must have sensed his deep devotion and respect for others, and William was drawn to her, perhaps understanding her need for security. He fell deeply in love with her.

It was January 25, 1871, when the couple was married in the new Presbyterian church on Tuscarawas Street just west of Canton's square. Ida was lovely in ivory satin and point lace. Following a "grand" reception at the Saxtons' house on South Market Street, the young couple honeymooned in New York.

They returned home to the white frame house on North Market Street which Ida's father had given them as a wedding present. The Major continued his fledgling law practice while Ida prepared for frequent informal evening gatherings with other young couples of Canton.

Nobody ever heard Ida call her husband by any name other than endearments, such as "Dearest Love", My Precious" and "My Sweetest."

On Christmas day 1871, she presented her Dearest Love with a daughter. They named her Katherine, after Ida's mother, and called her Katie. William McKinley was happier than he'd ever been in his life. His wife was radiant and his beautiful blonde daughter was an absolute joy to him. But this happiness was not to last.

In the early spring of 1873, just before the birth of the McKinleys' second child, Katherine DeWalt Saxton died. The shock of her mother's death was more than Ida could handle and that may have been partly responsible for the complications she suffered during and after the birth of her second baby, little Ida.

Mrs. McKinley was seriously ill. Specialists were called to examine her, she began to have convulsions or "fits," and when little Ida died before she was five months old, Ida suffered severe depression.

Pina took care of the toddler Katie, but Ida would not allow the child out of her sight, except to go riding with William. She often wept and clasped the little girl on her lap in a darkened room for hours at a time. Once when Abner came by, he found Katie swinging on the gate in front of the house. He invited her to go for a walk with him, but little Katie said, "No, I musn't go out of the yard or God'll punish Mamma some more."

Ida Saxton McKinley was an epileptic for the rest of her life. Her seizures were sometimes short and mild, but at other times, long and violent. Her illness changed the merry young woman McKinley had married into a "feeble, self-centered, nervous invalid." In addition to convulsions, she suffered blinding headaches, severe colds, digestive upsets and nervous problems caused by her menstrual cycle.

Blonde haired Katie, with the serious, handsome face of her father, was the only bright spot left in this home, but on June 25, 1875, exactly six months before her fourth birthday, Katie died.

Those who watched McKinley's activities from afar, could not know how much he suffered. He had been deeply hurt and became quiet and withdrawn.

At times he stared into space and forgot important testimony given in his court cases. Few knew his home life was teaching him the skills of a psychiatrist. Those who did know predicted in whispers that Ida would always be a "millstone around his neck."

If she was a millstone, William McKinley never seemed to realize it and never gave up hope for her recovery. He began to speak softly, ready at any moment to distract Ida from her depressed thoughts, as one would a small child.

He learned to shorten his stride to keep pace with her stumbling steps and to support her weight on his arm. He knew how to press her temples to relieve the throbbing pain in her head caused by an approaching seizure. Ida couldn't stand fresh air, but he never complained. He sat in stuffy rooms and rode in closed carriages to keep her comfortable and satisfied.

Although William was friendly, he was also a private person who never volunteered information about his wife's illness. When asked about her health, he would say one of two things: "she's feeling better," or "she's not so well today." This reserved answer discouraged further questions and, though his outward actions seemed to show indifference to her illness, he never left her alone except to take care of his professional duties. At the first sign of a seizure he was alert, ready to throw his handkerchief over her contorted face until the seizure passed.

Ida's beautiful face became strained, and her eyes either glared with pain or were dulled by sedatives. She couldn't stand the weight of anything on her head, including hair, so it had been snipped short.

This was the woman an ambitious and talented young man intended to escort to functions in Washington's society when he entered the race for Congressman from Ohio's Eighteenth Congressional District in 1875. The commitment he'd made to her was just as important to him as the one he'd felt toward his comrades in battle. He would take the best care possible of those placed in his life.

Despite Ida's appearance of poor health, she always seemed able to muster up the strength to do the things she wanted to do. Nobody knows whether she was as ill as she seemed, or whether she was an extremely insecure, jealous woman who used illness to keep her husband at her side. Nor is it important because it did not prevent William McKinley from reaching his goals in life.

He entered politics for the second time in 1874 when he campaigned on behalf of Hayes, who was running for his third term as governor of Ohio. In 1875, when Hayes was running for President, the Major ran for a seat in Congress. Ida's medical bills and the living expenses in Washington were both high, but McKinley chose to turn his Canton law practice over to his brother and partner, Abner, and to live on the smaller salary of a Congressman. His income included rental fees from the office building he had built in Canton on the southeast corner of Second and Market Street South, known as the "McKinley Block," which later housed the McKinley School of Law for twenty-six years.

When McKinley made his decision to become a politician, he realized that politics had become greedy. Many Congressmen responded only to the selfish interests of their own districts and ignored the welfare of the nation as a whole. It bothered William that nobody was working on the tariff, which he believed needed to be adjusted in order to make prosperity flourish in the entire country.

McKinley cringed at the spoils system which guaranteed well-paid jobs to unqualified friends and relatives of politicians who cared very little about public welfare.

During his 1875 campaign for Congress, he said:

> "Self-preservation is the first law of Nature, as it is and should be of Nations. 'General welfare' must come first. The country must be independent in a "broad and comprehensive sense, strong, self-supporting and self-sustaining. The Law of self-preservation calls for protection against inequality of cheap foreign goods."

The people of his district liked what he said and they elected him to a seat in Congress.

5

Handsome Young Statesman

When William McKinley Jr. took his seat in the United States House of Representatives in 1876, he was thirty-three years old. The farms and ranches of America were calm, but both industry and population were growing rapidly. Like the first awkward kiss of boy and girl, this rapid growth caused some embarrassment and frustration. Political and economic reforms hovered like kites over thickening clouds of national dissatisfaction.

Republican Ulysses S. Grant was President of the United States, and a victim of his own honesty and trust in others. He lost public trust because he either did not know about or chose to ignore the bribery and favoritism which existed within his administration during his two terms in office. During the election of 1876, violent charges of electoral fraud erupted over the twenty votes from South Carolina, Louisiana, Florida and Oregon, which were needed by both parties.

Congress recognized the profound anger of the public and responded to the accusations by appointing an electoral commission of fifteen men to choose the President. Since eight members of that commission were Republicans and they voted strictly along party lines, McKinley's old mentor, Rutherford B. Hayes, was chosen President.

At this same time, trouble with the Indians was sputtering out. The Sioux War of 1876 was one of the last serious attempts of the Indian to hold the land to which he had been born. It was late in June when the Sioux chief, Sitting Bull, led six thousand Sioux and Cheyenne warriors into battle near the junction of Big Horn and Little Big Horn Rivers in South Dakota. General George Custer and his six hundred soldiers died in a slaughter that was as ruthless as the Army's methods had been in its attacks on Indian villages.

That year, Americans celebrated the one-hundredth year of their Independence at Philadelphia's Centennial Exposition, where every important foreign country was invited to display its products and culture. The educational and cultural advantages of the Exposition were as valuable as its positive influence on trade among the exhibiting nations.

One of the educational exhibits displayed a device sent from Massachusetts by a young Scotsman named, Alexander Graham Bell. This first telephone was hardly noticed by the throngs of people who glanced briefly at it. It was the following year at Salem, Massachusetts, before anyone except for Bell, realized how his invention would revolutionize the transmission of sound.

In 1876, Congressmen were paid a salary of ten thousand dollars a year, and had to rent their own office space. Congressman McKinley found an apartment in the Ebbitt House in Washington, D.C., where he was able to rent a room across the hall for his office. He fully intended to stay as close to his ailing wife as possible, no matter where they lived or what his duties were.

The men who came to his office to conduct business with McKinley were often interrupted because Ida frequently sent for her husband. William never apologized for these interruptions.

While he was in Congress, McKinley focused his energy on the tariff problem and became its Congressional expert. Even though this tax on imported and exported goods was as old as history itself, it continued to be a very complicated problem.

Its far-reaching effects were less important to the ancient people of the world who could fill their needs from within the boundaries of their own land. As world trade increased, countries kept tariffs reasonably low so others would do the same. It was self-serving for everybody. In McKinley's day, American industry began to suffer loss of business because imports were sold to the American public for less than American-made products.

Public sentiment began to echo the ideas of the

Republican radical right-wing. To the radicals, it was a sacred tradition to be self-sufficient, and these isolationist beliefs spread across the country. People began to distrust the nations of the Old World and McKinley agreed that tariffs must be raised on imported goods in order to protect American business.

All of his boyhood experiences led to his support of the protective tariff. His birthplace had been named for Hezekiah Niles, a strong tariff defender. McKinley understood exactly how important it was to his father to receive a fair price for his product. He often mentioned the low-tariff years when his parents had scarcely enough money to buy food and clothing for their family:

> "Let England take care of herself," he urged his listeners. "Let France look after her own interests, let Germany take care of her own people, but, in God's name, let Americans look after America."

The philosophy of his political life was the same as that of his military and personal life. He had a deep reverence for the sanctity of "home," whether that home was filled with family, fellow soldiers, or fellow Americans.

During the time he studied shipping schedules and worked on his tariff ideas, other things were happening in the country which occupied some of his attention.

The workers who had built the railroads to the West and settled at the end of the line were angered by the influx of Chinese laborers. They complained that these immigrants worked twelve to fourteen hours a day for very small wages which deprived Americans of jobs.

When efforts were made to stop businesses from importing Chinese workers, businessmen took to smuggling them into the country. Finally, after serious riots in many western cities, President Hayes made a treaty with China to stop these immigrations. Some smuggling continued, but the major problem was solved.

A great step in modernization took place as the first electric street lamps were introduced by Thomas Edison in 1879, when he lit Menlo Park, New Jersey, with his latest invention.

It was also in 1879 that coins returned to American pockets for the first time since 1861. The use of coins as money (called specie payment) had been discontinued when the government issued *greenbacks* to finance the Civil War. When the return to coins was authorized in 1879, it was permissible to use either gold or silver in exchange for the greenbacks. The Department of the Treasury, however, traded only gold coins. This meant the country operated on an unofficial gold standard.

Silver miners were unhappy about this because the use of silver would have meant more sales for them. In 1879, the government promised to buy more silver but cancelled that agreement later.

McKinley supported the gold standard, yet his speeches and voting often carried middle-of-the-road tones about this issue. For many years the Republican party would not make an absolute choice between gold and silver, but kept one foot in each pot.

It was during McKinley's nearly 14 years in Congress, when Civil Service Laws came into existence. He heartily approved of these laws to employ qualified people.

In the meantime, Ohio's young Congressman continued to slave over the tariff. He became an expert at closing loopholes that foreign trade could slip through. He also learned how to increase the tariffs with bills worded in a way which appeared to lower the duty.

McKinley spent many hours listening to lobbyists argue against each other. All day they came to present their side of the argument and some came in the evening to be sure they had his full attention. His mind soon became well-stocked with every possible argument for and against tariffs. This information sharpened his tariff debating skills on the floor of Congress.

His quips of irony caused much humor on the House floor where he was never accused of being aggressive; rather, he was considered to be a talented diplomat. One of his friendly critics, Joseph Cannon of Missouri, accused him of keeping his ear so close to the ground listening for public opinion, that it was "filled with grasshoppers."

Grasshoppers or not, McKinley was a persuasive speaker who appealed to the good judgment and understanding of his listeners:

"The clear bell-like quality of his voice was magnetic to his listeners," La Follette wrote of him. "He spoke with dignity but with freedom of action. The pupils of his eyes would dilate until they were almost black, and his face, naturally without much color, would become almost like marble . . . a strong face and a noble head. When interrupted either in speech or debate, instead of seeking to put his man at disadvantage . . . he sought to win him. He never had a harsh word for a harsh word, but rather a kindly appeal: 'Come now, let us put the personal element aside and consider the principle involved.' "

In the Congressional election of 1882, McKinley was opposed by Jonathon H. Wallace, a lawyer who claimed he beat McKinley because he had more votes. The debate continued for nearly two years until May, 1884, when Congress voted to give McKinley's seat to Wallace. Ten months later, McKinley was returned to Congress by the voters.

McKinley was known to be a hard worker among his fellow Congressmen, but he was not familiar to the larger population of the Nation. In 1889, he won national recognition as the "champion of protection," with his increased tariff on imports.

During these fourteen congressional years, Ida McKinley hovered quietly in the shadows of life in Washington. She took cribbage lessons, cleaned jewelry and silver for others and crocheted slippers for friends.

Her closest friend was Lucy Hayes, wife of the President. Ida visited at the mansion and had lunch with Mrs. Hayes on two occasions without William. Once when the Hayes' spent two weeks away, William and Ida stayed at the Executive Mansion with the Hayes children.

Ida's poor health never kept her from going to formal state dinners when the McKinleys were invited, and she often had visitors at Ebbitt House. William did not socialize much. He spent most of his leisure time alone with his wife and they often went for the carriage rides she loved.

At Ebbitt House, he was in the lobby before seven o'clock each morning to get his mail and newspapers, then worked for two hours before eating breakfast with his wife. Every evening he could be seen strolling back and forth in front of the hotel while he enjoyed the after-supper cigar Ida disliked.

It was near the end of his congressional career, that William found himself ward of his brother James' two children, who were orphaned in 1889. The orphans, James and Grace McKinley, were brought back to Canton where William's mother made a home for them. McKinley was very fond of these two youngsters and was always generous in filling their needs.

The Congressman suffered a second personal loss a year later when his beloved sister, Anna, died July 29, 1890.

That same year McKinley was a candidate for Speaker of the House, along with Thomas B. Reed of Maine and Joseph G. Cannon of Missouri. McKinley wanted the speakership badly, but Reed had traveled widely and was well-read. He kept his diary in French and was the idol of some very cultured "highbrows." However, he was also a sadist who could quickly put others down with his caustic sneers. Some politicians were afraid of him because they believed his kind of wit was dangerous in politics.

McKinley would have been an excellent moderating Speaker, but at the time, the House Republicans needed an unyielding man in that position.

Reed won the seat; yet, recognizing McKinley's abilities, Congress made him chairman of the Ways and Means Committee, and majority leader on the House floor. Joseph Cannon and McKinley were appointed, along with Reed himself, as the three members of the Committee on Rules. This threesome made a powerful group controlling the House of the Fifty-first Congress.

The economy had slowly improved but when McKinley's tariff bill was passed in 1890, some unprincipled merchants raised the price of their merchandise long before the tariff could have caused the increase and the public blamed McKinley for the higher prices. Unknown to William, the Senate had also added trade agreements to his bill, the public agreed with the Senate, and McKinley had to back away from his former stance of isolationism. He never again pooh-poohed trade agreements after he found that the people and his party wanted them.

In the meantime, the Democrats had gerrymandered in Ohio and when it came time for McKinley to campaign in 1890, he was faced with unexpected resistance from constituents in the new areas of the Eighteenth

District who did not know him.

It was October, late to begin a campaign, but he set out to win back his votes. Day and night he rode the muddy roads of Ohio in wagons, and often times slept in the caboose of a train, in his effort to get to the towns and villages of his new constituents. The Democrats continued to use unethical tactics against him, but he worked doggedly to win the election.

He came too late and the Democrats won the election by a landslide. As often happens, McKinley's loss turned out to be the best thing that could have happened to him. Republican newspapers in Ohio claimed his campaign had made him more popular, and they predicted he would be the next governor of Ohio. Newspapers across the country echoed this praise and McKinley's name gradually became more familiar outside his home state.

The losing Republicans gathered around McKinley to bolster his ego and inflate their own, but many treated him as though he was inferior to themselves. Neither Joe Cannon, with his cute remarks about grasshoppers, nor any other of the smart politicians who thought McKinley was "common," could begin to guess how methodically this man was making plans to sit in the highest office of his homeland.

6

Ohio's Chief Executive

Marcus Alonzo Hanna, born in Ohio in 1837, was a wealthy businessman who attended Western Reserve College but did not graduate. He made his fortune in grocery, coal and iron sales by his aggressiveness.

He owned Ohio's prestigious Cleveland Opera House where he entertained other businessmen and politicians. Hanna was hungry for political power but wanted to be an unseen puppeteer. During McKinley's political life, Hanna became one of his friends and loyal supporters, though they did not always agree. Hanna liked men who protected business and he worked hard to remain in McKinley's favor.

McKinley did not possess the aggressiveness of Hanna and each man was comfortable accepting the benefits the other had to offer.

When McKinley lost his bid for another term in Congress, he listened to the overwhelming public opinion against the Tariff. He decided it was best to leave

Washington and considered that the governorship of Ohio might be a good place for a protectionist to wait for things to quiet down.

The governor's role at that time was limited to signing commissions and prisoner pardons. He had no veto authority, but McKinley, the eternal optimist, recognized this as yet another opportunity to sharpen his skills of debate.

When the movement for his nomination began, McKinley held back. He did not want to be defeated in his home state a second time and he knew Ohio voters were fickle in off-presidential election years. Only too often they voted for a Republican president, but chose Democrats in the elections between.

In addition to that, the Republican Party in Ohio had quarrelled and split during the 1888 gubernatorial convention. Joseph B. Foraker, then governor of Ohio, and Marc Hanna engaged in a bitter quarrel and each claimed a portion of Republican support. McKinley needed both men on his side and wisely stayed out of their quarrel, again waiting for things to calm down.

When spring arrived, the quarrel was over and McKinley had the united support of the Republican Party for his candidacy to the governorship. He asked Foraker, who was also an excellent orator, if he would make the nominating speech at the convention.

Foraker was delighted. At the Ohio Republican Convention in St. Louis, Missouri, that June, he presented such an enthusiastic speech that William McKinley Jr.

was nominated to run for Governor of Ohio by the excitement and applause the speech evoked. Foraker's wife, Julia, recorded that the cheering "kept up for thirty minutes. . ."

Hanna participated in McKinley's campaign for governor only by collecting money. He had the knowhow since he had collected funds for Benjamin Harrison's Presidential campaign in 1888. He collected money for McKinley's fund from Chicago and Pittsburgh, as well as in Ohio.

McKinley focused his campaign strategy on issues which gave him the national publicity he wanted. His leading issue was the gold/silver currency squabble. He searched for and found a position which made both gold and silver supporters happy and won him the governorship with a comfortable margin in an election that saw many Democratic winners. McKinley interpreted this Republican victory as public approval for both a "sound and uncorrupted currency" and the Tariff policy he'd worked so hard for in Congress.

In his inaugural address January 13, 1892, he tackled the problem of the "mere figurehead" governorship head-on. "I shall have the opportunity, Gentlemen of the General Assembly," he said, "of meeting you very often in the next two years and to political friends and adversaries alike, I desire to say that I trust our relations will be of the most friendly and agreeable character."

Those were not empty words. They were the

prophecy of an executive who would render improved service to the public by using his agreeable personality.

He went on in his speech to discuss the state's problems in realistic, well-informed terms with an emphasis on public welfare. The only comment he made about politics was to condemn the practice of changing boundaries of voting districts to get more votes for a predetermined party. He did not think this gerrymandering practice was fair.

Governor McKinley's father died November 24, 1892, during his first year as governor. After his father's death, McKinley dropped "Junior" from his name and changed his signature from William McKinley Jr. to William McKinley.

His first move as governor was to suggest spending cuts to the legislature and to request authority to study tax changes because state finances were in such poor condition. He was given permission to appoint a commission to study ways of increasing state income without taxing personal real estate and other property that already carried a full tax burden.

The commission recommended, among other things, a franchise tax on corporations. Foraker was angered at the idea of taxing telegraph, express, and telephone property and when the bill was introduced to the legislature, both he and Hanna worked hard for its defeat. McKinley kept his comments about this new tax neutral. He asked for more remedies and promised a more fair method of taxing, but never referred to corporations in a specific way.

The Governor believed these small taxes on business were justified by the state's low income, and the public agreed. McKinley praised the legislature for their marvelous ideas and stressed the need for even more reforms.

The philosophy for fairness McKinley adopted during his early life was clearly seen in the labor laws that were legislated during his terms as Governor. Their greatest importance was their concession that laborers had a right to explain their grievances to a neutral board.

The acts designed to protect railroad and streetcar employees from accidents were the Legislature's response to another of the suggestions in McKinley's inaugural speech.

Another bill fined employers who tried to keep their workers from joining unions. McKinley especially supported an industrial arbitration bill that reflected recommendations he'd made while in Congress. Even though there was no way provided to enforce arbitration, many disputes were satisfactorily settled by his new arbitration board.

McKinley's popularity with both businessmen and working men of Ohio was proved when both groups contributed to funds for his second gubernatorial campaign.

However, when some of his most loyal supporters in Massillon, Ohio—the miners of Stark County, became violent and rioted in 1894, he put his foot down firmly.

The bituminous coal miners of Ohio's soft coal mines weren't satisfied with the progress of negotiations between the United Mine Workers and the arbitration board. The Massillon miners went on strike before John McBride, President of the UMW, called a general strike, and they remained on strike after other miners had settled. Their anger peaked when West Virginia coal was shipped on the railroad through Massillon to points across Ohio.

The enraged miners "seized and sidetracked the trains, stoned the crews, tore up rails and burned railroad bridges." Frantic sheriff's officers tried to stop further spread of the destruction, but finally sent telegrams to Governor McKinley requesting his help.

Preservation of public peace was the first responsibility in McKinley's code of duties and weighed heavier than either his "political cautiousness" or his hatred of using force. He sent for John McBride, whose union headquarters were across the street from the State Capitol.

"John," he said, "you have gone too far. If you don't stop it before evening, I will call out the entire National Guard of the State to keep the railroad running."

That afternoon McKinley notified officers of the National Guard to get their troops ready but he firmly instructed them the Guard was absolutely not to make any combat with the miners. He knew many of the guardsmen were relatives of the miners and he did not want bloodshed.

But he told Mr. Moore, his secretary, during the war he'd noticed there was "no fight if a brigade met a division." He believed numbers, not force, would win.

The first National Guard detachments were ordered out that evening. As the violence spread, McKinley sent regiment after regiment to the troubled areas. Peace came without the loss of one drop of blood and William McKinley's calm determination had won yet another victory.

The Governor received praise for prompt and courageous action, but the faultfinders rushed forward too. They complained that he was reckless and extravagant in spending tax money to pay so many troops.

The Chicago *Herald* said McKinley was on his knees asking favors from "desperados and outlaws." The Cleveland *Plain Dealer* said, "Bridge burners, train wreckers and highwaymen are usually shot on sight."

Most people did not form such harsh judgments and agreed with McKinley's temperate handling of the situation. The Canton *Repository* said it was only humane to prevent anarchy by milder means when possible. It was also critical of the mine owners: "If some coal operators in the craze of competition did not forget that coal miners are human beings, the expensive coal strike might have been averted."

Labor troubles in Ohio were not as serious as those in other states. The great Pullman strike in Illinios was especially destructive with fierce outbreaks of severe violence. This working class revolt alarmed the entire nation when streetcar strikers clashed with police, and as hungry Italians, Hungarians, and Poles continued to fight for jobs and organize marches to Washington.

The most famous—and most ridiculed of the marchers who went to Washington was "Coxey's Army." It was led by Jacob Silica Coxey of Massillon and was made up of shabbily-dressed, unemployed people who marched from Massillon to Washington D.C.

Coxey's idea was to create jobs for the unemployed by financing a bond issue to build roads. The unemployed would be paid for building the roads, but politicians laughed at his idea.

Those who ridiculed Coxey were not quite so smug that autumn when he ran for Congress as a Populist and took a lot of votes away from the Democrats in his district.

The economic crisis continued and McKinley stayed on his course of keeping peace and order. Each time a disturbance occurred, he sent the Military to subdue it without force. He told one group of threatening strikers: "I do not care if my political career is not twenty-four hours long, these outrages must stop if it takes every soldier in Ohio."

While most men in politics at that time earned the hatred of either conservative citizens or labor groups, William McKinley was able to keep the respect of both sides. This ability was seen by those outside his home state. His temperance and common sense continued to become more noticed in national political circles.

McKinley felt good about the improvements he was able to promote on Ohio's roads, canals, and institutions, and the open door policy he maintained in Ohio's Executive Chamber.

Public prominence had increased his dignity but did not destroy his country-bred simplicity. There was no sign of self-importance as he welcomed constituents into the high-ceilinged, wood-paneled Executive Chamber.

His visitors sat comfortably on deep sofas or easy chairs beneath a large electric chandelier where they could see portraits of the Ohio dignitaries which hung on the walls. He often broke his Garcia cigars in half and chewed them so as not to offend others with smoke. A large brass cuspidor sat near his massive desk in the middle of the room, and a cheerful fire often crackled brightly under the marble fireplace mantle.

McKinley's greatest political talent was his ability to identify with people from all walks of life. He never talked down to people; he spoke in terms everyone could understand. He was himself an average, middle-class man who was proud of his country, and who remained humble in his devotion to his past and his religion. McKinley could evoke the faith of the fathers in himself in all crises and was able to pull these same emotions from his listeners. Rich men, poor men, businessmen, farmers, merchants and workers all responded in the same way to this compassionate man.

The political arena in Ohio of that time was not called "dirty" by polite society. They referred to it as "dusty," but it was notoriously dirty. McKinley was able to work hand in hand with shameless bribery-givers and -takers who must have made his personal philosophy of honesty cringe inside him day after day. He carefully avoided all bribes and bargains himself.

William and Ida occupied a suite, first in the Chittendon, across from the State Capitol, then in the Neal House, during his governorship. Every morning before he entered the Capitol, he stopped and waved to Ida as she waited at the window to watch him enter the building. Each afternoon, at precisely three o'clock, McKinley stopped whatever he was doing to stroll to the window where he waved at her again.

As his governorship drew to a close in 1895, he began to look for a home to buy. It had been 20 years since he and Ida had lived in their own home and he was anxiously waiting for the time he could enjoy that lifestyle again.

They had sold their home in Canton when William became a congressman, but discovered it was available to lease again in the fall of 1895. Both were delighted, and after some quibbling about needed repairs with the owners, they rented it.

Ida wasn't up to the decorating chores, but a friend came to the rescue. New carpets, curtains, linens, blankets and china were ordered. Ida selected her own silverware—then began to plan a party.

She "set her head" to dazzle the people of Canton, while at the same time, she would show everybody she was strong enough to serve as First Lady of the land. After all, her illnesses didn't interfere with her hearing and she was fully aware of overtures the Republican Party was making to her husband about the next presidential nomination.

Elegant invitations to a silver wedding celebration were soon going by mail to Canton, Alliance, Pittsburgh, Youngstown, Cincinnati, Chicago, Cleveland and perhaps further.

On a dreary, warm day in early February, 1896, trains pulled into Canton's South Market Street depot, carrying elegantly dressed ladies and gentlemen, all heading for the celebration on North Market Street.

They went by horse and carriage, past the Saxton house, the *Evening Repository* building, and the Courthouse on the square. At Eighth and North Market Streets, they found the sidewalk carpeted from the gate to the porch. On the front lawn were two locomotive headlights to light the walk after dark.

An eight-piece orchestra played in the entrance hall to welcome them and enormous bouquets of roses, hyacinths and carnations were banked in each room.

They ate chicken or lobster salad, sweets, lemonade, coffee or claret, served by perky waitresses who carried filled trays to the serving tables. Caterers moved busily under the temporary canvas canopy over the back porch to keep the trays filled.

From three o'clock until five in the afternoon and again from seven to eleven o'clock that evening, Ida sat at her husband's side on the seat in the bow window of the parlor and received guests. Her face was haggard and her once lovely auburn hair was dull and cut short, but she held a massive bouquet of white roses on her lap and smiled graciously to welcome their guests. She wore her ivory-satin and point-lace wedding dress.

And William was happy to be home among friends and family again. He put aside, for the moment, thoughts of the presidency.

7

The Nation's Leader

Marc Hanna was a kind-hearted man but showed little restraint in the way he manipulated both men and circumstances for political gain. When he wanted favors from somebody, he took no short-cuts in flattering and grooming them. Hanna loved to host lavish breakfasts and weekend house parties for his political prey. Anyone even remotely important to his ambitions were often given tickets to the best box seats in his Cleveland Opera House to enjoy their favorite plays and musicals.

In 1895, Hanna began to introduce McKinley to influential southerners at carefully planned gatherings in his rented house in Georgia. While McKinley allowed himself the benefit of meeting Hanna's social contacts, he absolutely refused to use those benefits publicly. He said ". . . anything like seeking to promote my personal interests is very distasteful to me."

Many of the southern contacts McKinley made, both black and white, became admirers who were impressed by his sincere desire for North-South reconciliation. Thus, quietly and smoothly was born the presidential campaign of William McKinley, barely noticed by either press or politicians.

The campaign went public as "McKinley for President" clubs began to form. When he was invited and spoke in Hartford, Connecticut that spring, it looked like a break in loyalty to Thomas Reed, also a Republican presidential hopeful. Rumors began to circulate that McKinley's New England speech was a bid for the presidential nomination, which upset William. He made sure that he didn't call attention to his plans again.

Politician Asa Bushnell had given McKinley ten thousand dollars to help repay the creditors of the tin plating fiasco and McKinley owed him. William threw himself into support for Bushnell's campaign for governor of Ohio, warmly welcomed him as Governor, then retired to Canton.

The house on North Market Street was busy with activity as his presidential campaign got under way. A telephone hung on his library wall, telegraph messages zipped in and out, and notables came to visit.

Newspaper reporters from large and small cities hung about on the front porch hoping for tid-bits of news. Ida entertained with stories of her youth, her love for children, and her romance with the Major, from her seat in the bow window of the parlor. One Philadelphia reporter saw "the steel badge of courage" in Ida's eyes, and documented her impression that Mrs. McKinley would be able to manage White House entertaining.

Marc Hanna provided money, organization and publicity for McKinley, who was never able to advertise himself. Critics have called this "excessive modesty a flaw."

But Nancy Allison McKinley showed this same kind of reluctance to brag. Once when she was going to Columbus by train to visit her governor son, a fellow passenger asked where she was going. Her humble, unrevealing reply was, "To Columbus to visit my son."

Ida was not strong enough to travel a campaign trail, William refused to leave her, and true to form, he found a compromise. He campaigned from the porch of the house on North Market Street, and the presidential campaign of 1896 became known as "The Front Porch Campaign."

The citizens of Canton enjoyed the excitement as people from all over the country stepped off the train to sing, march and wave flags on their way up Market Street in ever greater numbers. By the end of September, the crowds numbered twenty to thirty thousand, and McKinley was making up to sixteen speeches each day. He thoroughly enjoyed the eight weeks of this festival atmosphere, while restaurants, hotels, and saloons bulged, as did their cash registers.

The visitors carried or wore every possible kind of campaign paraphernalia. There were gold-headed canes, buttons, hats, banners and flags. McKinley wore a "gold bug" in his lapel as he pushed hard for the tariff and spoke for the gold standard:

> "That which we call money, my fellow citizens, and with which values are measured and settlements made, must be as true as the bushel which measures the grain of the farmer, and as honest as the hours of labor which the man who toils is required to give."

McKinley won the presidential election by a large popular majority. His entry into the presidency was handled with greater courtesy in Washington than had been seen before. President Cleveland invited him to a dinner on the eve of inauguration which Ida did not attend. She rested in a brass bed with a pink canopy.

The morning of the inauguration, March 4, 1897, was clear and breezy. Both Pennsylvania Avenue and the park east of the Capitol—where a platform had been built for the ceremony, were packed with people.

Ida wore a royal-blue velvet gown with Renaissance lace on the bodice, a black toque bonnet edged in white and a short sealskin cape. She looked ill, as she staggered down the steps with the help of Secretary Porter.

William's relatives were all in attendance, including his energetic, independent 87-year-old mother, who strolled about with an armful of roses she'd gathered from the dining tables on the train.

But nine months later, tragedy struck the woman who had always been called a "peacemaker." Nancy Allison McKinley suffered a stroke December 2, and died December 12, 1897, at her home at 131 West Tuscarawas Street in Canton. She was buried with her husband, William Sr., and children, James and Anna, in

Westlawn Cemetery, Canton, Ohio.

The Bible text McKinley took to Washington with him was from the Old Testament: Micah; Chapter 6, verse 8: *"He hath shewed thee, O man, what is good; and what does the Lord require of thee, but to do justly, and to love mercy and to walk humbly with thy God?"*

His inaugural address touched on three main topics: a balanced budget, the industrial depression, and a reference to the Cuban problem, of which he said, "We want no wars of conquest. We must avoid the temptation of territorial aggression."

President William McKinley came to the White House with some unique qualities for that time. He shaved every morning when most men still copied Abraham Lincoln's example and sported beards of various descriptions. McKinley brought to his dealings with Congress a polished diplomatic skill which few Presidents have ever possessed and he was the last Civil War veteran to serve the Nation as its President.

The new President was gracious and friendly, but ever careful in dealing with people. He never foundered in the sticky mire of over-familiarity and was never heard to make a degrading remark about others.

His secretary at the White House, George Cortelyou, recorded in his diary and other records he kept, that William McKinley was a tolerant man. He pointed out that some of the domestic help in the White House didn't provide the best of service, but McKinley made only one change. He replaced the housekeeper whom out-going President Cleveland told him was "too frivolous and flirty."

Though McKinley had always taken care of the household chores for Ida, the Nation's problems were of much greater concern to him in 1897, and he left household complaints to staff members, with one exception. He insisted that everyone who dropped in at White House social affairs was welcome. He did not permit any "class snobbery," much to the aggravation of the household staff, who found it difficult to plan food and drink orders. Guests often complained of overcrowding at these functions, but President McKinley only smiled and continued to chat with everyone who came.

The Cuban revolt against Spain had surfaced again in 1895, and Americans were becoming increasingly huffy about Spanish cruelty to the Cubans, the loss of Cuban trade, and the threat to American-owned lands in Cuba.

There was renewed interest in an American-built canal through the Isthmus of Darien in Central America to provide speed and safety for shippers, but Great Britain continued her refusal to cooperate.

The threatened extinction of seals in the Bering Sea by Canadian fur hunters was a growing concern. Russia, Japan, Canada, the United States and Great Britain were all involved.

In the Pacific Ocean, Great Britain, Germany, and the United States were having trouble with the three-power protectorate over the Samoa Islands which had been formed in 1889.

The Hawaiian government was asking to be made a Territory of the United States because Japan had recently taken a lively interest in those islands.

Beyond the Pacific, China was being threatened by the French, and Russia was trying to take over Japan's interests in Germany, Great Britain, and Manchuria.

At home, there was widespread industrial depression, the national debt was increasing, Civil Service Laws needed to be strengthened, and fear was spreading that the gold standard would not be sustained.

McKinley chose to "put (our) own house in order first." He stressed the need for: passage of a protective tariff, immediate adequate revenues with a balanced budget, control of industrial disturbances, and a change in the financial system.

He said, ". . . revenue must come first by an adequate taxing system." In his characteristic style, he approached these complex problems with simplicity and common sense. It is doubtful the American public recognized the excellent judgment which lay behind his words.

The Tariff of 1897 confirmed McKinley's statement that the revival of business would "depend more largely upon the prompt, energetic and intelligent action of Congress than upon any other single agency affecting the situation." Congress had acted by passing this bill, which raised tariffs to higher levels than ever before and the country prospered.

The question of Hawaii's annexation was settled when the final resolution making her a Territory of the United States became law in 1900.

In 1897, McKinley had also appointed a commission to study and present plans for a Nicaraguan Canal. Great Britain refused to grant the United States exclusive rights for control of such a canal until 1901, when the commission's plans finally moved toward becoming a reality.

Civil Service laws were strengthened in 1899, and became even more effective in rooting out the old spoils system.

The President wisely postponed consideration of the single gold standard until the last half of his administration. By that time, Japan and Germany had both established a gold currency, and McKinley recommended all greenbacks redeemed in gold "shall be kept and set apart and only paid out in exchange for gold."

Congress followed his suggestions when it passed the Act to establish these gold reserves March 14, 1900. This idea of McKinley's was one of the most important financial reforms in America's history because it separated the questions of income from currency stability.

The greatest challenge of McKinley's life and administration lay in the Cuban crisis, which ended in the long-threatening, but short-lived Spanish-American War in 1898.

Spain had ruled Cuba from 1492 when Christopher Columbus claimed the islands for her. The original Arawak Indians who lived in Cuba soon died off from overwork and disease. Cuba was then re-populated by Spaniards whose descendants were called Creoles.

In 1762, England seized the islands but returned them to Spain when the Treaty of Paris was signed in 1763. The years between 1763 and 1895 were filled with periods of Cuban revolts against Spanish suppression. These later years were also filled with turmoil and revolution in Spain itself.

When the 1895 eruption occurred in Cuba, the island natives were rebelling against the Spanish categories of four classes of people, and they wanted independence.

The population was divided as follows:

1. The Spaniards, born in Spain, who occupied offices and positions of power.

2. The Creoles, who were planters, businessmen and lawyers.

3. The free mulattoes and negroes, about 1/6 of the population, who were not permitted to hold office.

4. The slaves, 1/3 of the population, who were mere chattels.

Nearly all Creoles, mulattoes and negroes were deprived of freedom of speech, press, religion, and education. They were heavily taxed to support a Regular Spanish Army on the island plus a large army of Spanish officials, who received huge salaries, and who routinely robbed civilian Cubans.

When the Cubans revolted against this suppression, Spain immediately ordered the army to destroy plantations, sugar cane, plantation buildings, and the plantation railroad connections. The revolutionists responded by burning and destroying crops and real estate, also. Soon many old people, women, and children had no place to live, and they died from disease and hunger.

Americans who owned land and lived in Cuba were either put in prisons or killed, and as death and destruction continued, the American people at home wanted it stopped.

President McKinley agreed with those who said the United States had a greater obligation to humanity than to Spain. He disagreed with those who wanted to jump into war too quickly because he believed Spain should be given every chance to leave Cuba peacefully. He was also painfully aware that the United States Army and Navy were not prepared for war.

McKinley had to take a lot of abuse from both Congress and a press that was accused of inflaming the American public against Spain, for his slow response to the situation. The President stood solid in his convictions. He refused to expose American boys and their families to the suffering of war unless there was absolutely no other solution.

Supplies for war were ordered and soldiers were enlisted while the President patiently and wisely prodded Spain for peace. But Spain was proud and didn't want to give up the islands she'd ruled for more than four hundred years.

At first, the Spanish rulers pretended to agree to peace, but President McKinley learned the agreement was a treachery, designed to make the United States pay Spain all the money she'd spent in Cuba. Shortly afterwards, on February 12, 1898, the *USS Maine* blew up mysteriously in Havana Harbor and sank with more than two hundred American men drowned or killed.

Still the President worked for peace. He looked old and tired as worry and sleeplessness etched deep lines on his face. He often paced the floor in the Oval Office until after midnight in search of answers to the crisis.

"McKinley told Senator Fairbanks, 'It isn't the money that will be spent nor the property that will be destroyed, if ever war comes, that concerns me, but the thought of human suffering that must come in the thousands of homes throughout the country is almost overwhelming.' "

McKinley made his final plea for peace to Spain on March 26, 1898. When this failed, he notified Congress on April 11, 1898, that all diplomatic attempts of the government had failed.

"In his speech to Congress he said, 'In the name of humanity, in the name of civilization, in behalf of endangered American interests which give us the right and the duty to speak and to act, the war in Cuba must stop. The issue is now with the Congress.' "

Congress promptly accepted the responsibility and declared war with Spain on April 26, 1898. The war lasted just one hundred and thirteen days. Spain sent a letter of surrender dated July 2, 1898, with the following conditions:

1. Spain would relinquish all claim to Cuba and would leave Cuba immediately.

2. Spain would cede Puerto Rico and other West Indies Islands to the United States.

3. The United States could occupy and hold the city, bay and harbor of Manila in the Philippine Islands.

President McKinley wasn't satisfied with that. He was concerned about the Filipino people. He believed it would be cowardly and dishonorable to permit Spain to keep the Philippines because she had suppressed others too much. The islands couldn't be given to the French or Germans, who were commercial rivals of the United States; that would be bad business. The Filipinos couldn't be left to themselves; they weren't ready for self-government and this could only result in anarchy and misrule worse than Spain's had been.

He asked that Spain give the Philippines to the United States to pay for the destruction of Americans' property in Cuba, but offered to reimburse the Spanish government for internal improvements and public works it had built in the Philippine Islands. The United States would try to "educate, uplift, Christianize, civilize and do our very best" for the Filipino people.

The final peace treaty was signed in December, 1898. The United States was given control over Cuba, the Puerto Rican Islands and the Philippine Islands to continue until the inhabitants were able to develop successful self-rule. The sincerity McKinley showed in wanting to help these people become independent nations won him world-wide respect.

President McKinley ended his first presidential term with the respect, not only of Americans, but of all nations. The public liked his open-door policy and his lack of self-importance and high-browed pretense.

McKinley was the Republicans' unanimous nominee for a second term, but the choice of the Vice President led to much debate because McKinley refused to allow Marc Hanna to choose his running mate. Though Hanna was thoroughly upset, Theodore Roosevelt was chosen with McKinley's approval.

The fact that McKinley was deeply disappointed in Marc Hanna never became well-known and critics claimed McKinley was Hanna's pawn. This view is contradicted by McKinley's conduct in the White House.

One evening, Charles Dawes stopped by the White House on his way from a Republican dinner which Hanna had attended. "How did Hanna handle himself?" McKinley asked. Dawes answered with the parable of the rooster who believed his crowing made the sun rise each morning. The President did not make a comment, but smiled. That facial expression was the only criticism he ever made of Hanna, but those who knew McKinley well, knew he was deeply irritated by people such as Hanna, who exaggerated their own importance.

Marc Hanna, in his busy arrogance, probably never

realized he did not have the President's approval and he continued to yield to McKinley's tact and diplomacy.

When McKinley accepted nomination for a second presidential term, he made it very clear—this would be his last political office.

In July, 1899, he bought the home on North Market Street back and told Cortelyou:

> "We began our married life in that house, our children were born there, one of them died and was buried from there. Some of the tenderest memories of my life are centered there and some of the saddest. I am as happy as a child to have it back. It's a fine old place."

The election campaign of 1899 found Americans content with their government. The bitterness and divisions of the Civil War had been replaced by cordial feelings between North and South.

When McKinley took his oath of office for the second time, it was as the leader of a reunited nation. He was returned to the Presidency with the confidence and good will of men in both parties.

The problems he faced at the beginning of his second term were: to continue prosperity, to control trusts by careful monitoring of monopoly formations, and to protect small businesses.

A more personal problem, a plot to assassinate President McKinley, was discovered in 1900. The scheme was originated in Patterson, New Jersey, by a group of anarchists who planned to kill six rulers of the world in a predetermined sequence. The first two had already been murdered and McKinley was fifth on the list.

McKinley went ahead with his normal plans and, accompanied by some of his Cabinet members and their wives, he and Ida left Washington by train April 29, 1901, for a tour of cities in the South and West to discuss current national problems with the public at town meetings.

Ida developed an extremely painful felon, which had to be lanced, on one of her fingers and the infection spread into her bloodstream. The tour continued for a time, with parades and speeches in various towns, but McKinley abandoned the trip in Monterey, California, and took his wife to San Francisco.

Ida became bed-ridden and was so ill she sank into a coma for a time. A physician in San Francisco diagnosed her illness as an infection of the lining of her heart caused by the bacteria from her finger infection. McKinley never left her alone, which was not unusual. Marc Hanna once said, "President McKinley has made it pretty hard for the rest of us husbands here in Washington." Though his friends always knew of his devotion to his invalid wife, now the entire country learned how much he gave up for her. When he prayed for her recovery, the whole country prayed with him.

Recover she did. When she was able to travel, McKinley's plans to attend the Pan-American Exposition in Buffalo, June 12, were cancelled, and the train took them directly back to Washington. On July 6, William and Ida returned to Canton where Ida recuperated for two months. President McKinley calmly and confidently rescheduled his appearance in Buffalo for September. But his wife, bravely and silently, tried to push away troubling forebodings.

8

"Don't Let Them Hurt Him"

Ida supervised the packing for the trip to the Exposition with deep unrest. During that day, Tuesday, September 3, 1901, she told William she didn't want to go nor did she want him to go. She felt so strongly about it that she made an entry in her diary that night saying she wished they could stay home.

The President's secretary also had misgivings and tried to persuade McKinley to cancel the public reception. McKinley's comment was, "Why should I? No one would wish to hurt me." Mr. Cortelyou pointed out that there would be hundreds of thousands of people and it would be impossible to shake hands with everyone, to which the President responded, "Well, they'll know I tried, anyhow." George Cortelyou sighed and telegraphed Buffalo for more police protection.

William's optimism prevailed, as usual, and on Wednesday, September 4, 1901, the special train carrying the presidential party arrived in Buffalo, New

York.

The next day William delivered an address from the Esplanade at the Exposition to an enormous crowd. He said:

> "God and man have linked the nations together. . . . no nation can longer be indifferent to any other. Let us ever remember that our interest is in accord, not conflict and that our real eminence lies in the victories of peace, not those of war."

The crowd of American people, high United States officials, and representatives of foreign countries applauded him warmly and sincerely, not knowing it was for the last time.

Friday, September 6, 1901 dawned bright and sunny in Buffalo. The President, his wife, and party rose early, breakfasted, then boarded a special train to Niagara Falls. After viewing the Falls, the group took carriages for a trip around the area and drove halfway across the suspended bridge where they could look across to Canada.

It was a very warm day and the President changed his perspiration-soiled collar during the return trip to Buffalo after lunch. He took extra handkerchiefs because they soiled quickly as he frequently wiped perspiration from his face and neck.

The presidential party arrived at the Exposition grounds from their trip at three-thirty. Ida was sent by carriage to the Delaware Avenue home of John G. Milburn, president of the Exposition. The President kissed his wife, watched the carriage as it moved away and waved to her several times before he stepped back to join Mr. Milburn and Mr. Cortelyou. The three men purchased a cool drink, then strolled to the Temple of Music where the reception was scheduled.

The furniture in the auditorium at the Temple of Music had been rearranged for the President's reception line to open a wide aisle between the decorated chairs. This wide aisle was essential so that guards could have a clear line of vision to watch every person who approached the president.

A large frame in the corner behind where the President would stand was covered by a large American flag flanked by tall, potted plants. In addition to looking nice, it would also prevent an attack on the President from behind.

When the President arrived at the building, the organ began to play the national anthem, and the line of expectant hand-shakers stirred and applauded as he made his way to the corner prepared for him.

When the guards moved into position, the wide aisle was narrowed with the additional men who had been provided, and the first rule for presidential protection was broken.

The second break in those regulations occurred when the guards didn't enforce the rule that any person who walked toward the President must have both hands clearly visible and empty.

It was very warm, people had stood in line in the hot sun and handkerchiefs were frequently seen as people wiped their faces. Nobody even noticed a young man's right hand wrapped in a handkerchief.

The procession of people entered the auditorium through a door on the east wall, moved past the President, and out a door on the opposite wall as a Bach sonata sounded dimly through the commotion.

President McKinley was relaxed and smiling, especially enjoying the children. At four o'clock, when Cortelyou gave the signal, the east door was closed and those inside began to hurry to see McKinley.

A short, slender, clean-shaven young man, dressed in a black suit, had been standing near the door since the President arrived, but nobody noticed him. When the door was closed, the young man hurried along close behind the last person in line. As the man in front of him shook hands with the President, then moved aside to leave, the young man extended his bandaged right hand.

The President looked sympathetically at the bandaged hand, smiled at the mild-looking man, and reached out to shake his left hand. At that moment, two pistol shots cracked sharply from a revolver hidden in the bandages.

A thin veil of smoke wafted between the two men as Secret Service Agents grabbed the assailant and shoved him to the floor. People screamed, the young man was dragged to the center of the room and somebody punched him squarely in the face. Bayonets were drawn to keep the horrified and angered crowd back.

At this time, the President was being helped to a chair, but he saw the angry punch by one of the Secret Service men, and heard the anger in the crowd. He paused briefly and said in a pitying tone, "Don't let them hurt him."

The ambulance was summoned and while they waited, friends fanned the President with their hats, but McKinley wasn't thinking of himself. He was worried about Ida and whispered to Cortelyou, "My wife. Be careful, Cortelyou, how you tell her. Oh, be careful."

Four minutes after the shots were fired, the ambulance arrived to take the President to the Emergency Hospital on the Exposition grounds. As he was carried into the small building, he spoke again to Cortelyou, "It must have been some poor misguided fellow," he said.

The doctors found that one bullet had been deflected by a button or some other item and had only scratched the skin. The other one went through his stomach and was still lodged in an unknown place in his body.

McKinley was prepared for surgery and as they began to give the ether anesthetic, he recited part of the Lord's prayer, "Thy Kingdom come, Thy will be done, for Thine is the Kingdom with the power and glory forever. Amen."

The surgeons sutured the two lacerations in his stomach, removed blood from around his stomach and intestines, then closed the skin and applied a sterile dressing. They did not put a drain in the wound, and antibiotics were not yet discovered.

President McKinley was taken by ambulance from the hospital to the Milburn residence still under the anesthetic. Ida waited patiently to see him and when she did, she surprised everybody with her strength. She leaned over him lovingly and held the helpless hands—those which had been her strength for so many years.

During the night, the President aroused from the anesthetic in a house that had quickly changed to a hospital-hotel. The stables had become an executive office with telegraph equipment, and the house next door housed clerks and stenographers called from Washington to handle the overwhelming numbers of cables and telegrams.

The street was closed to traffic, barricades were manned by police, and a detail of soldiers patrolled the sidewalks on the block. Several tents and an election booth were erected opposite the Milburn house for members of the press.

Ida was permitted to visit her husband on Saturday, and by Monday his temperature was coming down, he'd been given some nourishing liquids, and medical bulletins were hopeful. They reported that if no complications arose, recovery would be rapid. Hope began to ease the fears of a nation.

The President had scheduled a reception for Thursday, September 12, and since he was improving, it was decided to go ahead with those plans except that the program would be changed to a service of Thanksgiving.

When Thursday came, McKinley was in good spirits, had no pain, his mind was clear, his temperature was down, and his pulse, though somewhat rapid, was strong. The Buffalo physicians were not as optimistic as those from Washington, but the Thanksgiving service was held as planned. When it was over, many government officials returned to their homes in Washington immediately afterwards. Vice-President Theodore Roosevelt went to a place in the New York mountains, ten to twelve miles from a phone.

The very next day McKinley suddenly became worse. Gangrene had moved—unnoticed—along the path of the bullet and now showed itself. The President's heart began to fail and the heart stimulants the doctors gave him were useless.

Late in the day, he called the doctors to his bedside and said, "It is useless, gentlemen. I think we ought to have prayer." The dying President recited the Lord's Prayer, then asked for Ida.

She came to him, kissed his lips and begged him to take her with him. William put his arm across her shoulders and said, "It is God's way. His will, not ours, be done." Quiet descended on the couple as they held each other for awhile, then the President whispered, "Nearer, My God, to Thee."

Those were the last words Ida was to hear him say. Attendants took her away as McKinley sank closer to death. During the next hours, the President seemed to slip in and out of consciousness. Occasionally he moved his head on his pillow and whispered, "Oh, dear."

Somewhere in the shadowy house a clock chimed. It was two o'clock Saturday morning. Fifteen minutes later, William heaved a long, labored gasp for air. Silence followed. Dr. Rixey leaned over, placed his stethoscope on the stilled chest, raised his head and said, "The President is dead."

Bells tolled in the night to tell the world the sad news and Saturday morning was met with widespread grief and fear. Grief for the loss of their President and fear for the future. People had learned to trust this man, to believe in him, and now they worried about their prosperity and the ability of an unknown man named Roosevelt, to fill McKinley's shoes.

A guide had to track Vice President Roosevelt up Mount Marcy to give him the telegram that told of McKinley's relapse. Roosevelt scrambled down the mountainside, rushed over mountain roads all night and at dawn on Saturday, in a small railway station, learned of McKinley's death. He climbed aboard the special train which waited for him and secluded himself inside a car where he remained, refusing to speak to anyone, until he reached Buffalo.

Theodore Roosevelt went immediately to the house of mourning to pay his respects, then made his way to Ansley Wilcox's library to await his induction. Ellis Root, the Secretary of War, brought Judge John R.

Hazel to administer the oath of office.

Slowly a small group gathered in the dimly lit room, made more bleak by summer dust covers over the furniture. Lyman Gage, Secretary of Treasury, and John Hay, Secretary of State, were both in Washington, but the other Cabinet members stood in the library with a few officials, guests, and members of the press.

Root tried to make a tribute to the late President but his voice was choked. Finally the oath was administered and President Theodore Roosevelt delivered the short response that Root had suggested to calm the fears of the nation:

> "I will show the people at once that the administration of the government will not falter in spite of the terrible blow . . . I wish to say that it shall be my aim to continue, absolutely unbroken, the policy of President McKinley for the peace, the prosperity, and the honor of our beloved country."

The Nation mourned. Newspapers carried a black bar across the front page; flags in every city, town and hamlet flew at half-mast; and the strains of McKinley's favorite hymn, "Nearer My God, To Thee," carried on breezes around the flags and buildings wherever people gathered.

The World mourned. In the Philippine Islands, one speaker said, "America has lost in the person of McKinley the first of her sons and the Philippines a friend who would have opened for the country, the doors of life."

"A Filipino editor closed his column with the words, 'We, the Filipinos, as the best offering, lay upon the tomb of President McKinley, faith in America, trust in the Republican doctrine.' "

Cables poured into Washington from every nation of the world, expressing horror at the assassination of William McKinley.

And from the Indian Congress of the Pan American Exposition came a message McKinley would have cared deeply about, but it received little attention from those he left behind. Seven hundred braves and their four leaders, Chiefs Geronimo, Red Shirt, Blue Horse and Flat Iron, sent a crudely lettered, cardboard card with a wreath of purplish evergreen. Their words were:

"The rainbow of Hope is out of the Sky. Heavy clouds hang about us. Tears wet the ground of the tepees. The paleface too are in sorrow. The Great Chief of the Nation is dead. Farewell! Farewell! Farewell!"

A funeral service was held in Buffalo on Sunday, and on Monday, the flag-draped mourning train moved slowly to Washington D.C., where the body lay in state until Wednesday. At noon Wednesday, the coffin carrying William McKinley's body arrived in Canton, Ohio, for formal services and burial on Thursday.

The people of the nation were so engrossed in their own sorrow that Ida was left to suffer alone. She cringed helplessly in the corner of her seat on the train during the long trip between Buffalo and Canton.

One of the last entries in her diary is dated, Friday, September 20, 1901. It says:

"I do not want to live if I can't go with my Precious to heaven above where all is love, there will be no sorrowing there."

Ida did not attend the funeral or the burial of her Beloved at Westlawn Cemetery in Canton. When McKinley's casket was carried out of the house on North Market Street at three-thirty in the afternoon on Thursday, Ida cowered in bed.

The Nation was silent. Trains, streetcars, boats, buses and businesses came to a standstill for five full minutes as a united people bowed their heads in homage to this great Statesman.

Ida never recovered from her loss and she died May 26, 1907.

The words of Benjamin Ide Wheeler, President of the University of California, who bestowed the degree of Doctor of Laws on McKinley in the spring of 1901, are inscribed on the pedestal of McKinley's statue in front of the McKinley National Memorial in Canton, Ohio:

"WILLIAM MCKINLEY, PRESIDENT OF THE UNITED STATES: A STATESMAN SINGULARLY GIFTED TO UNITE THE DISCORDANT FORCES OF GOVERNMENT AND MOULD THE DIVERSE PURPOSES OF MEN TOWARD PROGRESSIVE AND SALUTARY ACTION. A MAGISTRATE WHOSE POISE OF JUDGMENT WAS TESTED AND VINDICATED IN A SUCCESSION OF NATIONAL EMERGENCIES. GOOD CITIZEN—BRAVE SOLDIER—WISE EXECUTIVE—HELPER AND LEADER OF MEN. EXEMPLAR TO HIS PEOPLE OF THE VIRTUES THAT BUILD AND CONSERVE THE STATE, THE SOCIETY AND THE HOME."

Illustration by Mary Miller

President William McKinley, Jr., in Buffalo, New York.

9

"... Some Poor, Misguided Fellow"

President McKinley's assassin was Leon F. Czolgosz who was born in Detroit, Michigan in 1873, the fourth child of Polish immigrants. The family had moved often, following the work his father found as a laborer. When Leon was 12 years old, his mother died after giving birth to her eighth child.

Mr. Czolgosz remarried and settled his family near Pittsburgh, Pennsylvania for awhile, then moved to Cleveland, Ohio. They were very poor, but as Leon and his five brothers reached working age, the family saved enough money to buy a small farm and a store near Cleveland.

During childhood, Leon appeared to be normal. As a young man, he worked at a Cleveland wire mill where he was an exceptionally good worker. Fellow workers found him neither friendly nor quarrelsome. He was a loner, read radical papers and magazines, and attended some Socialist meetings.

The philosophy of Anarchism interested him. He came to believe that all rulers were enemies of the people, and began to hate the American system of government.

In 1898, when he was 25 years old, he had a nervous breakdown, quit his job, and went back to live with his family on the farm. Here he continued to be antisocial, going off alone to shoot small game, or putter with machinery. He was highly irritable and fought with his stepmother constantly.

As time went on, his mental state became worse. He began to fix his own meals, refused to eat with the family and took his food to his room. He read newspapers and magazines avidly, and was so fascinated by a newspaper story of the assassination of Italian King Humbert that he carried the article to bed with him for weeks.

Leon's irritability increased until the spring of 1901, when he became violently set on leaving the farm. He insisted the family should give him the money he'd paid out for the farm. In July the family finally paid him some of the money he demanded and he left home.

He wandered around the upper Mid-West, seeking Anarchists and attending their meetings. When his requests to join their groups were ignored, he moved to West Seneca, New York, which had a streetcar line to Buffalo. After several weeks at a boarding house, Leon made a quick trip to Cleveland and on August 31 he returned to Buffalo. This time he rented a room for two dollars a week over a saloon in the very center of the city.

Leon jostled around town, alone and unnoticed, for nearly a week. Nobody remembered having seen the young man, who said he was at the Exposition and heard McKinley's speech of September 5. After the shooting he told police he did not "believe that one man should have so much service and another man should have none."

The "misguided fellow" calmly went about buying a small revolver and, in the secrecy of his room, practiced the art of concealing the weapon in his hand with a handkerchief bandage.

He explained to investigators that he followed the presidential party to Niagara, but he'd planned to shoot the President during the afternoon reception.

When he returned from Niagara, Leon said that he shuffled through the crowd at the Exposition to the Temple of Music with the gun in his pocket. On top of the gun was a coarse-woven white cotton handkerchief. Visions of glorious martyrdom must have filled his mind as he planned this shooting where he knew he would be seen and caught.

Leon gave the investigators an alias. It was Fred. Fred Nieman, Fred Nobody. He had decided that, today, Fred Nobody would really be somebody.

For Leon F. Czolgosz, alias Fred Nieman, alias Fred

Nobody, justice came quickly. His trial began September 23, 1901. It was the "model of dignity, deliberation and consideration" for his legal rights.

The aged and highly respected Judge Loran L. Lewis concluded his assigned defense of Leon in a trembling voice with the words:

> "This trial is a great object-lesson to the world. Here is a case where a man has stricken down the beloved President of this country. If there was ever a case this is one. His death has touched every heart in this community and in the whole world, and yet we sit here and quietly consider whether this man was responsible for the act he committed. I had the profoundist respect for President McKinley. I watched him in Congress and during his long public career, and he was one of the noblest men God ever made. His death was the saddest blow to me that has occurred in many years."

The speaker's voice broke during his last sentence and tears flowed freely down his face. In less than one hour, the jury returned a verdict of "Guilty."

On October 29, 1901, Leon Czolgosz, the 28-year-old "poor, misguided fellow" was executed at New York's Auburn State Prison for the murder of the Nation's President.

10

"Skeletons in The Closet"

Every family has, at one time or another, a member or two who cause embarrassment, and sometimes agony. The McKinley and Saxton families were no different.

Abner McKinley learned the same lessons from the knee of the same mother as William did, yet, Abner never seemed to be as honest as William.

Abner's family life was highly honorable but a cloud of suspicion hung over his business dealings. When he lived in New York at the Windsor Hotel on Fifth Avenue, he also had a summer home at Somerset, Pennsylvania and maintained a lavish lifestyle.

Rumors floated around that he printed telegraph stock, sold worthless railroad bonds, and tried to sell stock in a company which made artificial rubber in the dark. "That's when they put the rubber in," people told each other jokingly. Abner was such a popular, well-liked man, most people shrugged his ventures off. They said he was gullible and simply a victim of sophisticated entrepreneurs.

Abner was in Washington frequently during William's presidency, where he coaxed favors such as the use of private cars, from White House personnel. One newspaper charged he was trying to promote himself within government agencies.

William ignored his brother. He never spoke of Abner's antics, never offered him public office, and never permitted him to touch one cent of public money. Though there was little criticism and no clearly defined law breaking, William must have suffered private embarrassment over this youngest brother and some of his shady dealings.

Ida's brother, George D. Saxton, created humiliation and agony for his family. He was a bachelor, notoriously fickle in his dealings with women. "Love them and leave them" seems to have been his motto as he relentlessly trod on the hearts and reputations of many women in Canton, Ohio. He was known as a "middle-aged Lothario" (a gay seducer of women).

George got more than he bargained for when he tangled with a pretty Canton dressmaker, Mrs. Anna George. He talked her into leaving her husband and two children, paid for her divorce, then tried to dump her. It didn't work.

She and her ex-husband kept after him for six years with a series of vicious law suits and counter suits. The last suit was filed by Mr. George charging Saxton with alienation of affection, and was settled October 4, 1898.

In the meantime, George Saxton was entertaining himself with a new mistress, Eva Althouse. On October 7, three days after the last suit was settled, George Saxton preened himself in the early autumn evening, hopped on his bicycle and rode to Eva's.

She wasn't home but he didn't know that, and he didn't see the figure hiding in Eva's bushes as he parked his bike, crossed the sidewalk, and started up her front steps.

The waiting figure in the bushes raised a gun and emptied it into George Saxton's abdomen. Neighbors heard the shots and ran to their windows to see a tall, slim woman in black standing in the shrubbery. Anna was arrested in short order.

Canton's residents felt sorry for the Saxton family, but little sympathy existed for the murdered womanizer. They believed that Anna George was the wronged person and poured their sympathy out for her.

She was serene and dignified during the following months of her indictment and trial. She steadfastly denied the first-degree murder charge and refused to answer questions from the county prosecutor.

In April, 1899, her trial ended. Spectators filled the courtroom and spilled onto the street outside. All agreed she was guilty, the jury deliberated twenty-four hours, returned a verdict of "not guilty," and the spectators cheered wildly for Anna. She left the courtroom and Canton, a free woman.

Though Ida suffered a great deal of anguish over this, she publicly reacted to the whole affair, including her brother's death, with indifference and did not follow the mourning tradition. She pretended to know nothing about it and threw herself into entertaining her friends with parties.

11

Ancestors

WILLIAM McKINLEY ANCESTORS

Abstracted from Olcott, family obituaries, and a folder in the files at the McKinley Museum in Canton, Ohio.

PATERNAL ANCESTRY

I. David McKinley (David, the Weaver) married Esther ________. Purchased 300 acres overlooking Susquehanna River in York County, PA. in 1743.
Had son:

II. John McKinley married Margaret ________.
Had son:

III. David McKinley married Sarah Gray, the daughter of John Gray and Hannah L. Stevenson.

Had son:

IV. James McKinley married Mary "Polly" Rose.
Had son:

V. William McKinley Sr. married Nancy Campbell Allison.

MATERNAL ANCESTRY

I. John Allison married Jean Brownlee.
Had son:

II. Gavin Allison married ___?___.
Had son:

III. Abner Allison married Ann Campbell, daughter of Obadiah Campbell.
Had daughter:

IV. Nancy Campbell Allison married William McKinley Sr.

The following brief family history has been published by Olcott as William McKinley's ancestral history, but has not been proved so far as can be determined by this writer:

The name of McKinley underwent several changes in spelling before the future president was born.

In 1547, at the Battle of Pinkie, a Scot Highlander, who spelled his name Ionlay, was killed defending his country. He had four sons who took the name MacIanla (Mac meant "son"). His oldest son, William used the spelling of "MacKinlay."

The sons of William MacKinlay settled in Perthshire, Scotland. Four generations later, one of William's great-great grandsons, James MacKinlay, called "James the Trooper," went to Ireland with the army of King William III and fought in the Battle of the Boyne on July 1, 1690. He stayed in Ireland and was the ancestor of the Irish MacKinlays. James had a son David, called "David the Weaver," who immigrated to America and bought three hundred sixteen acres of land in York County, PA in 1743. David changed the spelling of his name to McKinley when he came to America.

Bessie White Smith did not identify her source, but said of the paternal family of William McKinley: ". . . genealogists have placed one of them as the twenty-first in direct line of descent from the valiant Macduff, thane of Fife, who, according to Shakespeare, paraded upon the stage with Macbeth's head upon a pole."

12

Quotes

John Hay, Secretary of State:

"Probably no other President has been in such full and cordial communion with Congress, if we may except Lincoln."

Senator Cullum, who knew members of Congress in Lincoln's time:

"Even President Lincoln had difficulties with the leaders of Congress in his day, but I have never heard of ever the slightest friction between Mr. McKinley and the party leaders in Senate or House."

Senator Root:

"He was more thoughtful of others than any man I ever knew."

Marc Hanna, businessman, Senator, friend and adversary of William McKinley:

"He had little to say of the serious and sad things of life, but was always an optimist and his enthusiasm was infectious."

Charles S. Olcott, biographer:

"McKinley was always able to inspire sympathy for human suffering."

"McKinley earnestly labored for the workingman with not a suspicion of the hypocrisy which characterizes politicians who love the workingman for something in return."

"McKinley was essentially a man of peace. He brought it to Cuba, Puerto Rico, the Philippines and helped in China."

"McKinley maintained, 'We need God as individuals and we need Him as a people.'"

John D. Long, Secretary of Navy:

At McKinley's Cabinet meetings ". . . there happy humor ran free, there we saw the simple goodness of his heart, the unaffected, eager desire to discharge his duty and to do right."

George B. Cortelyou, President McKinley's secretary:

"He is a man of infinite tact and I have seen many a dangerous situation smothered out by his good sense and quiet influence."

"He is the strong man of the Cabinet, the dominating force but with it all are such gentleness and graciousness in dealing with men, that some of his greatest victories have been won apparently without any struggle."

A note found in McKinley's letter book in his own script:

"My belief embraces the Divinity of Christ and a recognition of Christianity as the mightiest factor in the world's civilization."

A Philippine speaker said that McKinley was: ". . . a man who was an enemy to the tyranny in the Philippines, and who, as a ruler, by his knowledge and tact, has convinced the people that the country where the American flag floats is a country where slavery and tyranny is an impossibility."

13

Memorials

ALASKA

Mount McKinley National Park*—established February 1917 to protect the herds of wild animals that roam the area. Located in south central Alaska, 120 miles southwest of Fairbanks. Contains nearly two million acres. Mount McKinley is at the southwest end of the park and is the highest peak in North America at twenty thousand, three hundred feet. Park season is June 1 to September 15.

CALIFORNIA

—San Francisco and San Jose

* The name of the park was changed in December, 1980 to Denali National Park. Denali is an Indian word meaning "Great One." Efforts to change the name of Mount McKinley to Mount Denali were not successful.

ENGLAND

Westminster Central Hall, London—Painting of McKinley

ILLINOIS

McKinley Park, Chicago—A semicircular granite exedra with McKinley's figure in bronze.

MASSACHUSETTS

Adams—A bronze statue eight feet tall on six-foot high granite pedestal with McKinley's left arm raised. Four bronze plates in the pedestal. One quotes his Buffalo speech, "Let us remember that our interest is in accord, not conflict, and that our real eminence is in the Victories of Peace, not those of War."

Springfield—McKinley's bust in bronze on a shaft of a sculptured female figure reaching upward with a palm branch in her hand.

MICHIGAN

Muskegon—Bronze statue of McKinley unveiled Memorial Day, 1902.

NEW YORK

Buffalo—

McKinley Monument, a sixty-nine foot monument made of Vermont marble with a twenty-four foot high base located at Niagara Square.

McKinley High School on Elmwood Avenue.

McKinley Parkway

The Victoria Club of Buffalo, composed of men of British birth or descent who sent a handwritten memorial to Ida McKinley dated September 16, 1901. ". . . But his martyrdom has merged all nations into one common family of sincere mourners, hard to be comforted, and the sad event has united all civilized people against their common enemy—that band of Red Handed Anarchists, whose theories and acts are as inscrutable as diabolical.
"Like his great prototype, who suffered for the sins of the world, President McKinley died forgiving his enemies and his last public utterances breathed Christ-like, goodwill and peace toward all men. . ."

OHIO

Canton—

McKinley National Memorial with Mausoleum of Pink Milford granite dedicated September 30, 1907. Statue of McKinley is nine feet, six inches tall and stands at base of Monument. Located in Westlawn Cemetery on McKinley Monument Drive N.W. Dedicated by President Theodore Roosevelt; statue unveiled by Helen McKinley, William's sister.

McKinley Museum of History, Science and Industry located on McKinley Monument Drive N.W.

The Stark County Bar Association adopted a memorial after his death as follows:

"His career at the bar gave ample evidence of that greatness of mind, purity of character, and kindness of heart, now known of all men, and of which his future career gave so many and striking illustrations. To every cause he gave a full measure of preparation. He was particularly distinguished as an advocate, presenting his cause to juries in such fair and just manner as to command their confidence and respect. To the Court, upon questions of law, he was lucid, strong, and convincing, never pressing an argument he did not believe in himself. To his adversaries, at the trial table, he was ever courteous and considerate, realizing that the objects of legal investigations are to arrive at the truth and subserve the ends of justice. He always aimed to keep forensic discussions upon the high plane of honest difference as to law of fact, and never indulged in personalities with opposite counsel or witnesses. To his colleagues, he was ever kind and considerate, always doing his share of the labor in a case, and never shirking responsibility or withholding from his associate the share of honor and praise which was his due."

Signed by: William R. Day, William A. Lynch, Joseph Frease, Ralph S. Ambler, James J. Clark, Frank L. Baldwin, David Fording.

McKinley School of Law—Established in 1926 by the Stark County Bar Association, and held classes in the McKinley Building that William McKinley built in Canton, Ohio until July, 1955, when the school was closed.

Canton Veterans Council—includes the American Legion, Amvets, Disabled American Veterans, Marine Corps League and the Army and Navy Union. Each year during the last week of January, this group holds a memorial program in honor of

William McKinley's birth date at the National McKinley Memorial in Canton, Ohio. In 1988, Army Reserve Brigadier General Bernard Losecamp placed the traditional wreath at the monument during the ceremony. Frank McCaulley, Department of Ohio Commander of the Army and Navy League, was the main speaker. Also attending were U.S. Representative Ralph Regula, R-Navarre; Richard Werstler, executive director of the McKinley Museum of History, Science and Industry and chaplain Harriet Bennett.

The William McKinley Visiting Scholar Program—Started through an initial grant jointly to Malone, Mount Union and Walsh Colleges by the First Endowment and Charitable Trust organized in 1967 by the Timken Company.

Church of The Savior United Methodist—120 Cleveland Avenue, S.W., Canton, Ohio

Four stained glass windows presented by Mrs. Ida McKinley in President McKinley's memory in 1907. The windows are: Joshua—God's Warrior, representing McKinley, the soldier; Moses—the Law Giver, representing McKinley, the lawyer; John—the Apostle of Love and Brotherhood, representing McKinley, the Humanitarian; and Cornelius—the Centurion, representing McKinley, the Statesman.

In the left center section of the Sanctuary is the pew which was occupied by President and Mrs. McKinley during worship services. It is marked with a commemorative plate and three needle-point cushions depicting a pictorial history of McKinley's life.

McKinley Avenue was dedicated in McKinley's memory on June 6, 1913.

McKinley Monument Drive was dedicated December 16, 1985.

McKinley Air Transport, Inc. located at Akron-Canton Airport.

McKinley Building at 403 McKinley Avenue, N.W.

McKinley Hotel Barber Shop at 213 South Market Avenue, located in McKinley Hotel, the building built by William McKinley, formerly housing offices and McKinley School of Law.

McKinley Life Care Center located at Eighth and Market Streets. See McKinley High School, Canton, Ohio, following pages.

McKinley Rifle and Pistol Club was originally the Canton Rifle and Pistol Club.

McKinley Theater at 901 30th Street N.W. (originally located downtown).

McKinley Title Agency, Inc. located in William R. Day Building on southwest corner of Cleveland Avenue and West Tuscarawas Street in downtown Canton.

McKinley Park at 510 High Avenue S.W.

McKinley Room located in Canton Memorial Civic Center - 1100 Market Avenue, North.

McKinley Wesleyan Methodist Church on Endrow Avenue N.E.

Stark County Courthouse, a painting of William McKinley hangs in one of the courtrooms.

Salvation Army Corporate Headquarters at 420 Market Avenue, South, has installed a round, leaded-glass window with a bust painting of McKinley which was given to them by the McKinley family many years ago. When it was found in the old building, it was cleaned, refurbished and installed over the front door of the new building. The door is angled so that the window faces the Saxton house on the opposite side of Market Avenue.

The window measures 4 feet 3 inches in diameter and is made of stained glass and hand-painted pieces joined with lead beading. It was given to the Salvation Army to commemorate the friendship between Ida McKinley and Evangeline Booth, the daughter of Salvation Army founder, William Booth. At first it was hung on the wall above the platform of the chapel in the original headquarters at 322 Walnut Avenue S.E. in Canton. When the headquarters were moved to Market Avenue in 1953, the window was hung in the lobby. Twenty years later it was given to the Stark County Historical Society and stored at the Historical Center. When Major R. Willis and Mrs. Elsie Muir became Canton's co-commanders in 1978, they felt it should be preserved and obtained permission to send it to the Army archives in New York for restoration.

The picture of William McKinley in the center of the window is hand-painted. Above his head is a hand-painted eagle, while on his right is shown the Salvation Army flag with the American Flag on his left. Stained glass pieces form a circle around the depictions.

The Ohio Educational Directory, 1987-88, shows the following schools in Ohio named for William McKinley:

McKinley Elementary School, Cincinnati
McKinley Elementary School, Cleveland
McKinley Elementary School, Elyria
McKinley Vocational Center, Findlay
McKinley Elementary School, Lakewood
McKinley Elementary School, Middletown
McKinley High School, Niles
McKinley Middle School, Portsmouth
McKinley Elementary School, Steubenville
McKinley Elementary School, Toledo
McKinley Elementary School, Warren
McKinley Elementary School, Willoughby
McKinley Elementary School, Xenia
McKinley Elementary School, Zanesville
McKinley Elementary School, Fairport Harbor
McKinley Elementary School, Lisbon
McKinley Elementary School, Poland Local School District, Mahoning County
McKinley High School, Sebring Local School District, Mahoning County
Columbus Linden McKinley High School, Columbus, dedicated in 1928.

Columbus—Statue of McKinley unveiled September 14, 1906, in front of the Capitol where he paused to wave at Ida each morning before entering the building.

Niles—McKinley Memorial Library with large statue at site of birthplace dedicated October 5, 1917.

Toledo—Bronze statue of McKinley making a speech stands on a granite base in front of the courthouse.

PENNSYLVANIA

Philadelphia

The Carnation League of America was formed in his memory.

McKinley High School in Canton, Ohio was dedicated to Anna McKinley, the oldest sister of William, who died July 29, 1890, and was a schoolteacher and principal in Canton for thirty years. The original school was built at North Market and Eighth Streets. The land was purchased in 1914, the cornerstone laid in July 1916 and the first half completed in 1918. Students from Central High School and North High School moved into the new building where classes began March 28, 1918 with eight hundred seventy-seven students. The auditorium and left wing were completed and the school was dedicated October 21, 1921. A new school was completed September, 1976, at 2323 17th Street, N.W. and the original school converted to the McKinley Life Center, dedicated to the care of the elderly and chronically ill.

TELL MOTHER I'LL BE THERE - Nancy Campbell Allison McKinley suffered a stroke December 2, 1897. When the President was notified by phone that his mother was ill, he said, "Tell Mother I'll be there." Canton residents of that time believed William McKinley wrote the song, "Tell Mother I'll Be There" which they sang on Mother's Day for several years after her death. However, that song has been found in an old hymnal at The Church of The Savior United Methodist Church at 120 Cleveland Avenue, S.W., Canton, Ohio, and was written by Charles M. Fillmore. It was inspired by McKinley's words, "Tell Mother I'll be there" and copyrighted as a renewal in 1924.

References

1. Blue, H.T.O., **History of Stark County**; The S.J. Clark Publishing Co., Chicago, 1928.
2. **Canton Repository**; issues from: 1871, 1875, 1890, 1892, 1893, 1894, 1895, 1896, 1897, 1898, 1901, 1940, 1943. Canton, Ohio.
3. **Cemetery Inscriptions, Volume VII**; 1986, by The Stark County Chapter of the Ohio Genealogical Sociey.
4. Foraker, Julia B., **I Would Live It Again**; New York and London, 1932 and 1975.
5. Leech, Margaret, **In The Days of McKinley**; Harper and Brothers, New York. 1959 and 1975.
6. **McKinley Museum of History, Science and Industry**. Canton, Ohio; files.
7. Olcott, Chas. S., **The Life of William McKinley**; Houghton, Mifflin, Boston, 1916, v. 1 and 2.

8. **The Church of The Savior United Methodist Church**; 120 Cleveland Avenue, S.W., Canton, Ohio. Hymnal. Copyright by Charles M. Fillmore, owner, 1924.
9. **The City Engineer's Office**, Canton, Ohio, 1988.
10. **The Land Survey Office**, Buffalo, New York, Howard Mandell, 1988.
11. **The Story of America in Pictures**; arranged by Alan C. Collins, Introduction by Claude G. Bowers, copyrighted by Doubleday, Doran and Company Inc., New York 1935.
12. Gene Noel, Principal; Columbus Linden McKinley High School, 1988.
13. McKinley Memorial Library, 40 North Main Street, Niles, Ohio 44446.
14. **The Boyhoods of The Presidents**; by Bessie White Smith, Lothrop, Lee & Shepard Co., Boston, copyright 1929.
15. Sharon Patterson, Librarian; Unity School of Christianity, Unity Village, MO 64065; Pamphlet, **"Tell Mother I'll Be There"** in files.

Index